Terry
Pratch

The Spirit of Fantasy

D0245645

Craig Cabell

Terry Pratchett
The Spirit of Fantasy

The life and work of the
man behind the magic

JOHN BLAKE

Published by John Blake Publishing Ltd,
3 Bramber Court, 2 Bramber Road,
London W14 9PB, England

www.johnblakepublishing.co.uk

www.facebook.com/Johnblakepub   facebook

twitter.com/johnblakepub   twitter

First published in paperback in 2012

ISBN: 978 1 85782 678 4

British Library Cataloguing-in-Publication Data:

A catalogue record for this book is available from the British Library.

Design by www.envydesign.co.uk

Printed and bound by CPI Group (UK) Ltd

1 3 5 7 9 10 8 6 4 2

Papers used by John Blake Publishing are natural, recyclable products made
from wood grown in sustainable forests. The manufacturing processes
conform to the environmental regulations of the country of origin.

Every attempt has been made to contact the relevant copyright-holders,
but some were unobtainable. We would be grateful if the
appropriate people could contact us.

This book is dedicated to the memory of Nigel Williams,
a dear friend and antiquarian book dealer who acquired many a
Pratchett novel for me

'The truth is that even big collections of ordinary books distort space, as can readily be proved by anyone who has been around a really old-fashioned second-hand bookshop, one of those that look as though they were designed by M. Escher on a bad day and has more staircases than storeys and those rows of shelves which end in little doors that are surely too small for a full-sized human to enter. The relevant equation is: Knowledge = power = energy = matter = mass; a good bookshop is just a genteel Black Hole that knows how to read.'
Terry Pratchett (*Guards! Guards!*)

'A ritual, more compelling than ever man devised, is fighting anchored darkness. A ritual of the blood; of the jumping blood. These... owe nothing to his forbears, but to those feckless hosts, a trillion deep, of the globe's childhood.'
Mervyn Peake (*Gormenghast*)

Acknowledgements

First I would like to acknowledge my dear friend and colleague Steve Moore, with whom I have discussed Pratchett's work and who was kind enough to read over the chapters of this book to ensure I didn't beat too far off the Pratchett track and to offer his own dose of wit and wisdom – many thanks for that.

Posthumous thanks to Nigel Williams, who had one of the most fascinating and value-for-money antiquarian bookshops in the whole of the Charing Cross Road area. Nestled in Cecil Court, Nigel acquired over a dozen Pratchett first editions for me, for which I am eternally grateful.

A big thank you to Colin Smythe, Terry Pratchett's agent, for casting an eye over the finished book and offering informed and detailed comment, especially clarity regarding early proof copies. Thanks also to Nathan for always wanting to 'acquire' the odd Discworld title from me, thus making me read them more quickly (although I did have to borrow the odd one from him too)! And thanks to Simon Gosden for finding a few obscurities for me and always being so amiable. Thanks to my dear friend

John Collins for keeping me up to date with the latest press cutting. (Next time my mysterious postman should stop for a small beer or glass of wine perhaps?)

I would also like to thank some dear old friends and acquaintances who pop up in this book in a variety of ways: James Herbert, Clive Barker, Stephen Laws, Simon Clarke, Joe Donnelly, Ian Rankin, Iain Banks, Neil Gaiman, Alice Cooper and Christopher Lee. Your influence stays with me, gentlemen, despite the passing years.

I would also like to thank some of the great fantasy writers past, such as JRR Tolkien, CS Lewis, Richard Adams, Robert Browning and the great Charles Dickens, who helped me realise the scope of the genre.

Thanks are due to Anita, Samantha, Nathan, Fern and my father Colin, for putting up with yet another book; Berny for the Terry Nation tip-off; and John Blake and John Wordsworth for allowing me to write about Terry Pratchett. Then there is my Danish friend Michael, who always uses Saturday morning football as the catalyst for varied conversation from Lord Nelson to Terry Pratchett – how diverse can you get? Thanks, too, to other members of the Saturday Morning team, specifically John and Robert.

Thanks to Tony Mulliken and those early breakfast meetings, which, as always, helped immensely.

Finally I would like to thank Terry Pratchett himself for being such a stimulating character to research and write about. His imagination and strength of character have brought so much happiness and hope to many people all over this world, and that is one of the fundamental reasons why I was so interested in writing this book.

Craig Cabell
London, 2011

Contents

The Wee Free Men
To Mad Hamish
Big wee wishes,
ye ken!
www.kidsatrandomhouse.co.uk/terrypratchett

A first edition of the first Nac Mac Feegle novel, inscribed in Pratchett's inimitable way

Introduction

(or what this book is and what this book isn't)

'... there are some things we shouldn't forget, and mostly they add up to where we came from and how we got here and the stories we told ourselves on the way.'
Terry Pratchett (Introduction, *The Folklore of Discworld*)

Strange things happen to you when you read Terry Pratchett's novels on the train. People bend over to study the cover and say 'I've read that one', which is really annoying. Even a ticket inspector has said that to me.

Pratchett's books are instantly recognisable nowadays, mainly for their impressive Josh Kirby dustwrappers. I know this because during a completely different train journey, I was reliably informed by a fellow passenger that somebody else was reading a book by the same author because the cover was 'bright and colourful and, well, quite similar, so it must be the same writer'.

There are fans of different characters within the Discworld series, from Rincewind and Luggage to Death and Granny Weatherwax, but perhaps more focus has been placed on Pratchett himself in recent years. Since December 2007, when he publicly announced that he was suffering from the early stages of Alzheimer's disease, Pratchett has spoken out about the affliction and his own personal plight. He has made a substantial donation to Alzheimer's Research UK, $1 million, and filmed a two-part programme about the disease for the BBC.* The confrontation he has had with his illness has won the hearts of many people, not just those who love his books, and he continues in his ceaseless quest to break down the stigma attached to the illness.

Pratchett has stated openly that he desires to take his own life when the Alzheimer's becomes too unbearable. He said he would like to end it 'sitting in a chair with a glass of brandy in my hand and Thomas Tallis on the iPod', and many people sympathise with that. Unfortunately the law is not a living, breathing human being and doesn't necessarily see it that way.

What I personally find fascinating about Terry Pratchett is his spirit, and it's that inner strength and ability to tackle the world full on which is the main theme of this book.

Terry Pratchett – The Spirit of Fantasy is *not* an unofficial biography and *not* a Discworld companion. It *is* a tribute to a man who has sold 70 million copies of his books worldwide in 38 languages, and who has shown that he wears his heart on his sleeve, even long before his illness. It is also a book that applauds a writer of fantasy whose very soul lives in the real world; and that's what makes him popular – his ability to make his audience empathise with his works and the real world around them.

It is not my wish to over-analyse and discuss the characters and plotlines of every Terry Pratchett novel in this book. A thousand words on each novel alone would be higher than the entire word

---

Alzheimer's Research UK is the United Kingdom's leading dementia research charity. It was founded in 1992 and is totally dependent on donations from individuals, not the government.

count available for this book, and would offer nothing new or insightful about the man or his works. So a different approach was needed, one that exposed relevant moments, situations and characterisations in his work against the backdrop of his life, philosophy and career, in comparison to the fantasy he writes. This may be frustrating for some Pratchett fans, who would like an in-depth analysis of, say, the Night Watch and the streets of Ankh-Morpork, but it is Terry Pratchett himself and how his work reflects the man that are important here.

Pratchett was knighted in the 2009 New Year's Honours. He had received an OBE in 1998 for services to literature, and many agreed that the accolade was well deserved by the much-loved author.

Pratchett's career as a novelist started long before *The Colour of Magic*, his first Discworld novel in 1983. His first novel, *The Carpet People*, appeared in 1971 and is hugely collectable in its first edition nowadays. But what do the early works tell us about the man, and how did they set the scene for the Discworld novels that followed?

There is more to Sir Terry Pratchett's life than Discworld, and this book makes that clear. Conversely, Discworld is so far-reaching, and the books and associated collectables so vast, that an extensive bibliography has been included at the end of the book (Annex C) for the incurable fan.* Not only does this provide a user-friendly checklist of items to acquire but also showcases the sheer volume of work Pratchett has produced and the amount of energy his publishers, agent and various artists have put into creating collectable editions of his works. This is also showcased in Annex A, in which I look at the films (mainly TV mini-series)

One must pay tribute here to Terry Pratchett's official website and to his agent Colin Smythe's website, which list a very comprehensive bibliography. I freely admit that I checked my own collection and other titles against these sites, along with claims of additional collectables; if items appeared to exist outside these official sources, I demanded to see evidence of their existence first.

made from Pratchett's work, which are all worthy of mention and are much-loved companions to the novels for many fans.

Terry Pratchett is one of the most respected fantasy writers Britain has ever produced. He's up there with Tolkien and CS Lewis, and one could not bestow a higher – or more relevant – accolade.

'No choice was left them but to play their part to its end.'
JRR Tolkien ('The Return of the King',
The Lord of the Rings)

A Serious Note on the Text

(and a bit of a rant)

Once upon a time Terry Pratchett's agent Colin Smythe walked into a well-known bookshop and asked where he could find the latest title by his author. Despite the book spending four weeks at number one in the bestseller lists, it couldn't be found in that part of the bookshop. Smythe was informed that it could be found in the science fiction/fantasy section, giving the distinct impression that books in that department were not worthy of the bestseller bookshelves, even though the title in question had outsold all other bestsellers for several weeks.

For me, it's not only the injustice that this narrow-mindedness conjures up, it is the superficial labelling of two genres under one heading. Although science fiction and fantasy do come under the umbrella of speculative fiction, they follow two different historical patterns. Fundamentally, science fiction has to be based upon a natural projection of current science, while fantasy doesn't need any of that but has a strong tradition of dwarves, warriors, wizards and dragons. The greatest visionaries in both genres are a million miles away from each other, people such as HG Wells and JRR

Tolkien, or Isaac Asimov and CS Lewis. People did believe once upon a time that there was life on Mars and so was born *The War of the Worlds*, but Wells' masterpiece says much more about the vulnerability and scientific naivety of mankind than just speculating about creatures from another planet, and that's what makes the book so valid today. Conversely, there is no Narnia at the back of the wardrobe, with fauns, talking lions and ice queens (well, not when I last checked), so *The Chronicles of Narnia* sit squarely in the fantasy genre.

One could argue that *The Lord of the Rings* created a history that has many parallels with our own great wars and great warriors, and involves the birth of a true language and the spirit of legend – stories passed down by word of mouth. But Hobbits are not based upon a scientific certainty, nor elves or walking/talking trees. *The Lord of the Rings* is a fantasy. I applaud its 'fellowship' and concede that the loyalty and honour Tolkien's great novel demonstrates is at the heart of every strong friendship in the real world, but dragons don't exist. On the other hand, Asimov's Foundation series was based upon political tensions in a science fiction setting. It is as cerebral as Wells' *The Shape of Things to Come*, but, unlike Wells' novel, impossible to film. Asimov, like Robert Heinlein, took politics into outer space and found an even more tangled web of intrigue and malice. One can argue that Pratchett weaves politics into his fantasy novels in much the same way, but the fundamental difference is that in science fiction it could conceivably happen because it is a forward projection, whereas in fantasy it can't, so it can only be satirical at best.

There is a discernible difference between science fiction and fantasy and that mindset is echoed throughout this book. Yes, parallels can be drawn between the two genres, but they don't necessarily have the same audience. TV's *Doctor Who* is not a fantasy series; it is a science fiction adventure series and has always been so. Conversely, a novel such as *The Neverending Story* cannot be classed as science fiction because it is an impossibility, something that can't come true in the real world, so it is fantasy.

Sometimes the speculation of the writer can be thought 'fantastic' even in the science fiction genre, but this is normally associated with the long-term vision of the writer. Again, HG Wells offers us a classic example with *The Island of Doctor Moreau*, where he predicts genetic engineering decades before it was ever dreamed of. Then there is Jules Verne and his breathtaking *20,000 Leagues Under the Sea*; the underwater ship – the nuclear submarine – dreamed up with accuracy.

It is important to understand that there are two genres within the forum known as 'anorak'. There are also two different audiences that cross over as much as those for detective fiction and historical fiction. 'And what of the horror genre?' I hear you cry. Yes, that sits next door to the double-header label of science fiction/fantasy in the high street, as it is also part of anorak heaven; but, oddly, horror fiction can sit on the bestseller shelves, so it is not as poor a relation as science fiction or fantasy in that respect. Not true? Consider this: a writer such as Clive Barker will write either a fantasy novel or a horror novel – never really a science fiction novel – and sit on the bestseller lists because he is known as a horror writer; just as Stephen King sat on the bestseller list with *The Eyes of the Dragon* and his Dark Tower fantasy series (and that's ignoring the fact that certain horror novels are now labelled 'chiller').

Some people will argue that science fiction and horror are the same genre, or complementary genres. Indeed, I have had many an unresolved discussion about that in my days at *Book and Magazine Collector*. Does *Alien* sit alongside *Do Androids Dream of Electric Sheep*? Strangely, yes – because both are science fiction. If the aliens murdering innocent people and breeding in a horribly grotesque way upset your delicate stomach, making you cry 'horror', then that is in itself ignoring the horrors of mother nature, such as the female black widow spider killing and eating her husband after mating. (Does the creature in *Alien* not behave, in some ways, like a black widow?) So science fiction is a fiction based upon science, and where's the horror in *The Hitchhiker's Guide to the Galaxy*? There are always crossovers, people pushing the boundaries, but essentially horror is horror, science fiction is science fiction and fantasy is fantasy. They all have their traditions, specific traits and audiences and one should accept that, or at least popular high-street bookshops should when stocking their bestseller shelves.

Going back to Pratchett not being on the bestseller bookshelves, let us observe that he is now. Like Stephen King, James Herbert et al, he is a fundamental part of the 'establishment' of authors who are now bankable products for the high street, but some genre writers are still being ignored. Why? A general feeling is that the problem is endemic in the UK. If a book is science fiction or fantasy it isn't taken as seriously as 'grown-up' genres such as crime and historical fiction. In the US that isn't the case, as science fiction and fantasy have a huge following and are taken very seriously. Also, the horror genre is turning slightly and becoming more true to life, which gives it more credibility and has sparked its offshoot of chiller fiction.

This book is about the fantasy genre and one of its greatest practitioners, Terry Pratchett, a man who has earned his place on the bestseller lists and is still continuing to break down the boundaries of his chosen genre.

> **'Science fiction is a subset of fantasy.'**
>
> **Terry Pratchett**

The above quote cannot be overlooked. I deliberately mentioned a science fiction show called *Doctor Who* earlier. Pratchett has written about this show in the past, and, although he claims that he watched the very first episode back in 1963 and enjoys watching the show today, he is quite appalled by how the Doctor can expound some fast-talking reason to explain how he has just saved the universe yet again. Pratchett goes on to explain that the logic behind some of the Doctor's solutions is just too 'fantastic' to be science fiction, so the stories are therefore fantasy. To my mind, this is where the genres get muddied. *Doctor Who* is set in outer space and is a children's science fiction adventure series (so more pace and less explanation are accepted). It is about an alien with two hearts, not in itself a leap of faith. His ship is bigger on the inside than the outside, an interesting scientific hypothesis, and he has the ability to change his appearance – to regenerate – when his body gets tired or damaged. OK, most of that is science fiction, but 'What about the regeneration?' I hear you cry. Let us consider a quote from one of the greatest writers of the macabre, Algernon Blackwood:

'The body, they assure us, changes its atoms every seven years or so, being therefore totally different at twenty-eight from what it was at twenty-one, but science does not commit itself with regard to mental changes, such changes being doubtless incommensurable... am I the man who wrote these tales so many years ago, or am I someone else?'

Algernon Blackwood (Author's Preface, *Selected Tales*)

I do agree that the sonic screwdriver is overused nowadays, but the main problem I have with *Doctor Who* is that it is disposable. Each episode is a rush against time that has to be killed dead in just under 50 minutes (or maybe two 50-minute episodes if you're lucky). The attention span of the television consumer has dwindled over the past 50 years. In the 1960s, *Doctor Who* could easily stretch a story over six or seven weeks (at least) in episodes of 25 minutes, but the present fan is apparently unable to cope with such frustrations. Life in the 21st century moves at a much faster pace; everybody wants their entertainment now. Music and movie downloads have made the younger consumer less patient: they don't need a lyric booklet with pretty pictures with their favourite CD, they just want the music on their iPod *now*; they don't want a hardback novel that has to be stored and loved, they want titles on their Kindle *now*. Things need to be done immediately, and society as a whole has begun to accept this.

As we move into a more computerised/virtual world, we find that taste is dictated by TV and word of mouth (that's if you can get the headphones off your friend in order to speak to them). People have become more insular, younger folk pinned to their bedroom laptops to prod a friend on Facebook, under-age youths assassinating criminals and Nazi zombies on PS3 then gloating about it on Skype, or texting their poor little fingers to oblivion (surely bad for teenage girls' fingernails?).

Traditional values are being reassessed. The LP lost out to the CD and now the CD has lost out to the download. Video lost out to the DVD, but the DVD has now lost out to the download too and, eventually, the time-honoured book will lose out to the download as well. But more obscure traditions are going too (evolving?). The photo album is no longer a tangible part of a family bookcase; it sits in a virtual library or on a computer back-up system. The wristwatch is now a digital display on everybody's mobile phone rather than a possession that sits on an individual's wrist. The downside to this latter change is that it's just a matter of time before children will not be able to tell the time on a traditional clock face.

Is what I'm saying science fiction? Indeed, some of it is. It is a forward-looking projection of the near future, but it is not a fantasy of the near future. That would be something like every house having a red dragon that told the time, televisuals plumbed straight into the consumer's head by organic scart lead and controlled by blue pixies listening to Led Zeppelin, and a flat Discworld sitting on the back of four elephants standing on the back of a great turtle swimming through space.

My analysis of different genres in this book is based upon the beliefs set out above. I apologise to high-street bookstores for any inconvenience caused, but there are defining lines within genres, and Pratchett knows that too. But, I hear you cry yet again: the turtle in the Discworld is travelling through space, so surely Discworld is science fiction or at least a strong crossover?

I totally disagree, because the fantasy outweighs the science fiction. There is no deep exploration of space across the Discworld novels. There are wizards (even a female one), witches, dragons, dwarves, goblins, and much more fantasy imagery than there are science fiction elements. To understand Discworld and the life and work of Terry Pratchett, you have to go to what is at the heart of his passion for writing and at the heart of his most important series – fantasy – otherwise nothing fantastic can come from any analysis of his life and works. And if the high-street bookshops refuse to place fantasy novels on the bestseller shelves, then they are clearly overlooking one of the most popular genres and not addressing the public's need for some extreme escapism in these troubled times. No wonder so many people now shop online. The ability to browse in bookshops will become a thing of the past, bookshops will cease to exist, and consequently people will become more insular – and less broad-minded – about their tastes. The eclectic consumer will become a thing of the past, so perhaps the fantasy novel will become an important genre, one that teaches people to use their imaginations again, to step back from the machines they so slavishly play with.

I recall the journal of the publishing industry, *The Bookseller*, calling for something to get children off computer games and, just when all seemed lost, up popped JK Rowling and the young Harry Potter. At that time, Pratchett was the country's most popular writer, but now we can say the top two writers in the country are both fantasy writers. And if that is not an interesting fact for you, witness the fact that Harry Potter books cannot be found in the science fiction/fantasy part of the bookshop, nor the children's section, nor even the general fiction department: they sit on the bestseller shelves.

It is important to have genres, to define what we as consumers want for our entertainment, and let us hope that the high street wakes up to the importance and popularity of the fantasy genre and gives it the respect it so richly deserves. Yes, people do have their own interpretation of what fantasy is, and that may muddy the waters somewhat, but if great works of fantasy are to be showcased, then there must be an area of the bookstore that is forever fantastic and that includes not just the latest sword-and-sorcery-titles but many of the books I list in the Further Reading section at the back of this book. There is more to the fantasy genre than meets the eye. Women didn't always wear tight black leather and ringlets; certainly not Alice in her wonderland, not Hermione Granger, and certainly not the women and children in Hamelin town by famous Hanover city!

'He started and rubbed his eyes. He had been so absorbed in the latter-day substitute for a novel, that he awoke to the little green and white room with more than a touch of the surprise of his first awakening.'
HG Wells (*When the Sleeper Wakes*)

Part One
The Road to Dreams

'... it is not our part to master all the tides of the
world, but to do what is in us for a succour of those
years wherein we are set, uprooting the evil in the
fields that we know, so that those who live after may
have clean earth to till. What weather they shall
have is not ours to rule.'

JRR Tolkien ('The Return of the King',
The Lord of the Rings)

CHAPTER ONE

Early On

Terry David John Pratchett was born on 28 April 1948 in the town of Beaconsfield, Buckinghamshire. He was the only child of David and Eileen Pratchett of Hay-on-Wye. Terry's father was an engineer and his mother was a secretary. In 1957 the family moved to Bridgwater, Somerset, for a short period, before Pratchett passed his 11-plus exams in 1959 and went to Wycombe Technical High School, Easton Street, High Wycombe.★   He could have gone on to grammar school but had no desire to follow the purely academic lifestyle.

In *Who's Who* Pratchett says he was educated in the Beaconsfield Public Library. This slightly flippant remark has an element of truth in it, as it was there he found his passion for books by reading fantastical stories. 'I became a reader at the age of ten and have never stopped,' he said. 'Like many authors, I read all sorts of books all the time…' What books? Pratchett cites

---

The school moved to Marlowe Hill in 1966, shortly after Pratchett left it, and is known today as the John Hampden Grammar School.

3

Kenneth Grahame's *The Wind in the Willows* as a major influence on his writing style, and one that has endured over the years. But once he got the reading bug, his appetite became voracious. He states that he had read all the James Bond books available to him by the age of 12, which was most of the original Ian Fleming titles at that time.

When he was old enough, Pratchett took a Saturday job in the local library. He wasn't paid for it, but, as he now jokes, they turned a blind eye to him having about '256 library tickets' – Pratchett left with two carrier bags of books twice a week. So the library really did become an important part of his education, as he recalls: 'One day the librarian handed me three books tied together with string, saying: "I think these will be completely up your street." It was *The Lord of the Rings*, which I read in one 24-hour sitting.'

The influence of *The Lord of the Rings* on Pratchett was immense. He describes his feelings of reading the book by discussing the prejudice in it. 'I remember always feeling sorry for the orcs... the elves always seemed to be up to something and the humans always seemed to fall from grace, but the orcs were the lowest of the low and beyond redemption.'

Pratchett has always had an enquiring mind. The way he questions the different species in *The Lord of the Rings* is in character with the way he distinguishes different cultures sympathetically in the Discworld series today.

> 'Rincewind had always liked boredom, treasuring it if only because of its rarity and value... The only time he could look back on with a certain amount of fondness was his brief spell as assistant Librarian at Unseen University, when there wasn't much to do except read books...'
>
> (*Eric*)

When one hears Pratchett recall his bookish youth, one begins to appreciate the grip books had on him and the process that led to authorship. 'It cannot be stressed often enough that before you can become a writer, you have to be a reader, and a reader of everything at that,' he states, and there is a lot of truth in that.

Although Pratchett read as much as he could in many different genres, it was two specific genres that left a lasting impression on him, as he recalls: 'It was science fiction and fantasy that got me reading and science fiction writers in particular have pack rat minds.'

'Rocket ships did not conquer space; they merely challenged it. A rocket leaving Earth at seven miles per second is terribly slow for the vast reaches beyond. Only the Moon is reasonably near – four days, more or less. Mars is thirty-seven weeks away, Saturn a dreary six years, Pluto an impossible half century, by the elliptical orbits possible to rockets.'

Robert A Heinlein (*Tunnel in the Sky*)

The exploration of space, as written by the great science fiction writers, combined with an early love of astronomy to set Pratchett's young mind ablaze. It is interesting to note that after his first novel (*The Carpet People*), his next two (*The Dark Side of the Sun* and *Strata*) are considered to be more science fiction than fantasy.

'There was no sound now in the observatory, and the lantern waned steadily. Outside there was the occasional cry of some animal in alarm or pain, or calling to its mate, and the intermittent sounds of the Malay and the Dyak servants. Presently one of the men began a queer chanting song, in which the others joined at intervals.'

HG Wells (*In the Avu Observatory*)

Science fiction writers opened Pratchett's eyes to other possibilities later on, as he explains: 'They introduced all sorts of interesting themes and ideas into their books, and so for me it was a short leap from fantasy and science fiction genres to folklore, mythology, ancient history and philosophy.'

If Pratchett's spare time was spent in the local library or secondhand bookshop (another favourite haunt of the youngster), what was he like at school? Children who read are normally the quiet, often bullied, members of the class, but Pratchett won most of his peers over by being the joker. He used his imagination to make up stories that made the other children laugh, which is often noted as being a quirk of a future writer. Pratchett recalls that he used to doodle and draw characters in his notebooks at school and sometimes he would also write quirky bits of text, some recalled years later as vignettes in his novels. However, one piece he wrote (which he can't now find) was a blend of JRR Tolkien and Jane Austen. He recalls a particularly good bit where the orcs take over the local rectory. So here we have an example of how developed Pratchett's quirky style was in his youth: we have his love of fantasy books, his love of writing, his keen sense of humour, but also, and most importantly, his desire to parody, mixing the greatest book of the 20th century, *The Lord of the Rings*, with a tried-and-tested literary classic.

> '**It was like being in a Jane Austen novel, but one with far less clothing.**'
>
> (*Nation*)

Did Pratchett do all this again with his first Discworld novel? No, he didn't. By that time he had moved on and was parodying the whole fantasy genre and only gently parodying characters from peerless classics.

Apart from providing Pratchett with a venue to entertain his fellow students with his literary attempts, how did Wycombe Technical High School develop his talents?

Pratchett recalls that it was noted on his school reports that he had a good imagination, but, as he jokes, the comments were normally written as negative aspects of his school life – comments like 'should pay more attention in class' instead of 'bound for literary stardom'. But the school also nurtured Pratchett's talents, as he wrote his first short story there at the age of 13 ('The Hades Business' in 1961), which was published in the school magazine. Pratchett's headteacher, however, condemned the moral tone of the story. Why? The basic plot was slightly subversive, especially for a child of 13: the Devil is having trouble recruiting souls for Hell, so he decides to get a business partner to create a theme park out of Hades, thus encouraging people to join. The Hades theme park becomes successful – so much so that the Devil decides to give up Hell and return to Heaven – just for a little peace and quiet.

To my mind, like so many of his short stories in the 1960s, there is an underlying message in the story if one wants to find it. Cheats never prosper, for example, could be a good moral pay-off for 'The Hades Business', so I'm sure the headteacher noticed something of merit in Pratchett's work.* Despite the headteacher's concerns, other stories followed in the school magazine, such as 'Solution' and 'The Picture'.* Two years later (in 1963), 'The Hades Business' was published in *Science Fantasy* magazine and with the money he made from this sale Pratchett decided to buy himself a typewriter.

Appearing in *Science Fantasy* magazine was a great

Some people also see a comparison with Pratchett's fourth Discworld novel *Mort*.

These two stories definitely appeared in the school magazine, but as Pratchett never kept copies of them, it is uncertain how many others were printed.

achievement. By August 1963 the magazine was in its 12th year and had won a lot of respect. Volume 20, No 60 (Pratchett's issue) boasted a short story 'Same Time, Same Place' by Mervyn Peake and an appreciation of Peake by Michael Moorcock. Pratchett's achievement of appearing in *Science Fantasy* magazine at the age of 15 is not one to be taken lightly.

The very act of submitting the story to *Science Fantasy* magazine shows that Pratchett believed in his own abilities and had a desire to be a published writer. Buying the typewriter proved his passion for doing so. Again, it is an impressive and very single-minded thing for a 15-year-old to do, but he remained level-headed about the future. 'When I was a little lad and thought about being a writer, I remember reading that the chances of making any kind of living at all from it were so low as to be negligible,' he recalled. But the dream was there.

> **'Like a child lost in the chasmic mazes of a darkening forest, so was Titus lost in the uncharted wilderness of a region long forgotten. As a child might stare in wonder and apprehension along an avenue of dusk and silence, and then, turning his head along another, and another, each as empty and breathless, so Titus stared in apprehension and with a hammering heart along the rides and avenues of stone.'**
>
> **Mervyn Peake (*Gormenghast*)**

Before the sale of 'The Hades Business', Pratchett had shown no real indication as to what he wanted to do in life. In retrospect, the move from insatiable reader to writer seems a natural one, but it was continued success that inspired him to consider a future as a writer. He wasn't being rejected, he was being encouraged.

Pratchett has described himself as a 'bolshy' kid. This is not to say that he was naughty, just a little headstrong. He knew his own mind and had a determination to see things through. This is echoed throughout his youth, from reading the whole of *The Lord of the Rings* in one sitting, to studying hard at school. He seemed to know instinctively what his priorities in life were.

So was Pratchett doing well academically? To a degree, yes; but, as he now explains, he did find maths a struggle, eventually parking an early ambition to be an astronomer because it meant you had to be good at figures.

He enjoyed more creative subjects. At school he loved lessons such as design technology (notably woodwork) rather than the more academic lessons such as maths and Latin. Outside school, Pratchett and his father were members of the Chiltern Amateur Radio Club (from the early 1960s), where their sense of humour was clear in their joint call sign: Home-brew R1155. So given the desire to play around with technology combined with a love of woodwork, one might expect that Pratchett seemed destined for a more practical career – not unlike his father – rather than writing. As it turned out, all these practical skills were nothing more than hobbies, as well as fuel for an active imagination.

The young Pratchett continued to do well at school. He achieved five O levels and started A levels in art, history and English, but he heard that there was a vacancy at the *Bucks Free Press* (a local newspaper). After consulting his parents, he went for the job and, remarkably, he got it, leaving school in 1965. When he got to the newspaper, he found that his education was far from over. He had to take a two-year National Council for the Training of Journalists proficiency course. He would come top in the country. If that wasn't impressive enough, he also passed an A level in English while on day release (his only A level pass).

Pratchett fell easily into journalism. He has described himself as a 'born journalist', and that the pleasure of hitting the keys as a touch typist is almost like a therapy to him. One cannot but agree, because in November 1965 Pratchett found his short story 'The Night Dweller' in a paperback anthology entitled *New Worlds SF*, edited by Michael Moorcock.★ 'The Night Dweller' is not considered a milestone in Pratchett's back catalogue. The few copies that come onto the market through antiquarian book dealers are often underplayed today and Pratchett fans are not exactly overcome with enthusiasm for the story either. What is interesting is the fact that Pratchett was still submitting stories for publication and, shortly after leaving school, he had had his second real success as a short-story writer.

Pratchett's drive, enthusiasm and natural ability had paid dividends again, and his talents as a writer of science fiction and fantasy did not go unnoticed at the *Bucks Free Press*. Very quickly he was given his own column, taking over 'Story Time with Uncle Jim' in the 'Children's Circle' section. Between 8 October 1965 and 17 July 1970, Pratchett wrote children's stories, sometimes in weekly episodes. In total he wrote 247 episodes, amounting to 67 individual tales, all fantasy stories but none of them with titles. They have never been anthologised in print but most are accessible on a website (www.terrypratchett.weebly.com), where they are now given distinguishing titles. Some of the stories can be viewed as pdfs of the original newspaper, or as text-only documents, whatever suits the reader. None of the stories were written under Pratchett's own name but they include Carpet People and other very Pratchett-like characters and situations, clearly showing the formation of the wit and wisdom of

---

Some people call this paperback *The Wrecks of Time* because the cover of the book depicts an interpretation of James Colvin's headline story inside.

Discworld years before it was conceived. When one reads the stories today, one can detect glimmers of the Pratchett we have grown to know and love over the years, so they are worthy of some analysis here.

> 'And, picking up their axes, they all walked off into the carpet, to chop down some big hairs to rebuild the village.'
>
> (Part one of an untitled story from the *Bucks Free Press*)

It was on 8 October 1965 that Pratchett began a 12-part series that is now known as the original version of *The Carpet People*. It starts with the ash falling from a human's cigarette, floating down to a thick carpet and being noticed by one of the Carpet People who is standing propped up against one of the carpet hairs, 'which to him was as big as a tree'.

Straight away the story is upon us, but then it needed to be. Each instalment of an 'Uncle Jim' story was no more than the equivalent of one side of typed, single-spaced, A4 paper in length. So Pratchett had to engage with his audience straightaway, and the name Uncle Jim and the caveat Children's Circle gave him clear parameters to work to.

There is something very Uncle Remus about Pratchett's tone, as if one expects Brer Rabbit to pop up at any given moment – but perhaps he does, as the whimsical characters are there. In the third paragraph of the first episode of that original version of *The Carpet People* story, he writes: '… the carpet was bigger than a forest, and was full of cities, towns and small villages, castles and all sorts of tiny animals, even cunning and hairy bandits in the really thick parts…' And there, 18 years before the first Discworld novel was published, was a flat world – a carpet – with fantastical creatures in a mystical – fantastical – setting.

CRAIG CABELL

Indeed, there is a fairy-tale quality to all of Pratchett's writing for the *Bucks Free Press*. In a way, he was recreating the Brothers Grimm short story, but without the menacing undertones.

The Brothers Grimm analogy is an interesting one, as the ancient folk tale was the origin of the fantasy story. Andrew Lang built upon this in a very late-Victorian type of way with his series of coloured Fairy Books, and Arthur Rackham built upon it even further by drawing and painting very sensual-looking fairies in anything from *The Fairy Tales of the Brothers Grimm* to *A Midsummer Night's Dream*.* Pratchett was fully aware of all this and embraced – and parodied – much of this history of fairy tale/fantasy in his works. Because he had studied it so well, he could avoid fantasy or dip into it whenever he wanted. But with the *Bucks Free Press* stories, perhaps he was still getting the traditional values of fantasy out of his system; indeed, he wallowed in them sometimes.

On 31 December 1965, he wrote a two-part story (concluding on 7 January 1966) about a factory. The first thing that we note is the tea made by the apprentice in the factory: spoons can stand up in it because it's so strong. There's some delicate humour here but also some hard lessons in life, because part one of the story ends with the realisation that the factory – which manufactures a certain type of pin (shades of a pin-loving postman from *Going Postal* looming here perhaps) – will go out of business because it can't mass produce its 'thrist pin'. In fact, it can only produce one a year, while the new factory across the road can produce 50,000 a second.

The 12 books that make up Andrew Lang's coloured Fairy Books are extremely important to the documentation of fairy stories. Most of the stories compiled by Lang had their first English-language publication in his books, with some translated by his wife. A full collection is extremely collectable in first editions. They are detailed in the Further Reading section of this book, along with other key works in the fantasy genre.

The moral of the story turns out to be that the one pin manufactured every year is used every year by the special machine that built it; nobody else anywhere needs such a pin. The company across the road had been built out of greed. They had failed to do any market research and found no demand at all for their product.

This very gentle but highly moralistic story has a similar blend of originality and morality as the best of Roald Dahl's children's novels, bearing in mind that Dahl's first bestselling children's novel was still about two years away.

Pratchett had instantly found a voice in Uncle Jim. He has since said that his career in journalism helped him as a novelist and this is clearly showcased through his Children's Circle stories.

Another important example of Pratchett's Uncle Jim stories is a one-episode story dating from 11 February 1966. It is significant because it demonstrates Pratchett's interest in historical events and twisting them to his own comic ends. It takes the Industrial Revolution as the setting for the story, turning Isambard Kingdom Brunel (the Victorian engineer of railways and steam ships) into Isombard Nuisance Funnel, the inventor of the Steam-operated House. Pratchett's sense of fun is there straight away, along with his ability to turn historical characters and facts on their head and create an ingenious, albeit very short, story into the bargain.

'What we must invent,' Funnel told the men in his factory, 'is something that will work a lot better than this new-fangled electricity, and costs a lot less.'

(From a one-episode short story,
Bucks Free Press, 11 February 1966)

We can see how Uncle Jim taught Pratchett to keep things tight and succinct, as dictated by the word count for each episode, and although little attention is given to his *Bucks Free Press* stories nowadays, one should not overlook them, if only for their endearing fun.

It is true that Pratchett's heart was firmly set on the fantasy and science fiction genres. He admits to watching the very first episode of *Doctor Who* on 23 November 1963, at exactly the same time he was reading so voraciously, so the combination of TV and literature was very important to him, as indeed was the cinema.

Every budding author is told to write about what they know, and Pratchett did that from day one. He had read *The Wind in the Willows* and *The Lord of the Rings* before sitting his school exams, and that awareness of the fantasy genre paid dividends when he began to write for the *Bucks Free Press.* His 'bolshy' attitude (let's call it determination) fuelled his desire to be a creative writer, even though he would not arrive at the Discworld series until 15 years later. By then, however, he was refusing to churn out tried-and-tested fantasy material – he had outgrown all those clichés and he wasn't afraid to say so.

> 'Lovers and madmen have such seething brains,
> Such shaping fantasies, that apprehend
> More than cool reason ever comprehends.
> The lunatic, the lover, and the poet,
> Are of imagination all compact.'
>
> **William Shakespeare**
> (*A Midsummer Night's Dream*)

CHAPTER TWO

What Happened Next

'I never expected to make money.'

Terry Pratchett

In October 1968, Pratchett married Lyn Purves at the Congregational Church in Gerrards Cross, Buckinghamshire. He was 20 years old and his life was moving at lightning pace. He was still writing his column for the *Bucks Free Press,* along with other news items and features. Shortly before his marriage he interviewed Peter Bander van Duren, co-director of publishing company Colin Smythe Limited. Van Duren had edited a book about how the educational system would look over the next ten years (*Looking Forward to the Seventies*). It was during this meeting that Pratchett told van Duren that he had written a novel called *The Carpet People* and wondered if he would consider it for publication. Van Duren said that they would be interested and passed the manuscript to his co-director Colin Smythe.

It didn't take long for Smythe to work out that they had a very talented young man on their hands, and he asked Pratchett to produce approximately 30 illustrations for his novel. Pratchett would draw and paint the illustrations throughout 1969 and 1970, and the book was published the month after his third wedding anniversary, in November 1971.

Smythe and van Duren wrote publicity material, the blurb on the inner flap of the book making it very tempting for younger readers: 'There is magic in every carpet. Cities and villages exist right under your feet and the people who live there are so small that each tuft of wool stretches high above them like great trees.'

Although they are becoming less common today, up until the new millennium it was almost standard practice for publishers to hold a book launch for new and important titles. Journalists, editors and freelance reviewers would be invited along to raise a glass or two to the new release and meet the author. The launch for *The Carpet People* took place in the carpet department of the upmarket furniture store Heal's on Tottenham Court Road in London. The trade turned up with their light blue invitations to the launch – the publicity folders had been illustrated by Pratchett – and were handed a cocktail called Essence of Underlay (the recipe for which, Colin Smythe tells us, is now lost). Large card images of the Carpet People were displayed in front of carpets in that department and Pratchett drew his characters on other sheets of card for the smattering of children who had accompanied their parents to the cheerful launch.

Pratchett also inscribed copies of the book for people, writing in Colin Smythe's copy: '... and may his book make lots of money! Best wishes, Terry, 16 September 1971'. He also hand-painted all the illustrations in Smythe's and van Duren's copies in beautiful watercolours, and added other doodles and comments as well.

The Carpet People was printed in a run of 3,000 copies. It had a black dustwrapper with a central colour image of the creatures of the carpet eating a grain of sugar, again drawn and painted by Pratchett. The hardback boards were two-toned bronze and green, making an attractive, but slim, volume.

Despite the enthusiasm for the book, there were not many reviews. The ones that were printed were very good but they failed to stimulate sales. Most copies of the book were sold to libraries, making fresh, untarnished copies very rare today. Some copies of the book were sold to North America and have the original British price of £1.90 clipped off. These copies are not worth as much as priced UK copies.

Copies of Pratchett's first novel remained in stock for many years, and were given new price labels until they eventually sold out. Pratchett collectors today keep an eye out for the super-rare copies of the book – no more than a dozen having colour illustrations painted by Pratchett, and only two known to have all the illustrations painted.

Pratchett has described his first novel as 'The Lord of the Rings of the microscope', and one can see in The Carpet People how ten years of feasting on fantasy novels had influenced his style.

What is interesting is that the young man didn't launch himself into a frenzy of novel-writing from then on. He was a journalist and enjoyed his job immensely; the writing of books was just a hobby for winter evenings. He enjoyed drawing and painting too, illustrating his own book being the culmination of a skill that he had started to develop by embarking on an A level in art back at school.

On 28 September 1970, Pratchett moved from the Bucks Free Press to the Western Daily Press. He would return to the Bucks in 1972, but this time as sub-editor. On 3 September 1973 he moved on again, this time to the Bath Evening Chronicle. He was still involved with Colin Smythe Limited, attending occasional book launches and drawing cartoons – he provided a series of cartoons for their monthly journal *Psychic Researcher* up until 1975. These depicted the work of the fictitious government paranormal research establishment Warlock Hall, and one can imagine that Pratchett would enjoy exercising his satirical flair in these cartoons. Pratchett illustrated about 17 issues of *Psychic Researcher* and these remain some of his most obscure contributions to this day.

It is important to note Pratchett's flair for art, from illustrating his first novel and drawing with children at his book launch, through to his cartoons in the *Psychic Researcher*. Today, the Josh Kirby dustwrappers to his books are eye-catching and as much a part of the Discworld series as the novels themselves, but one can instantly see a Pratchett character in the mind's eye, as if it has been drawn for you, so one should never underestimate the importance of art in Pratchett's life.

One could argue that Pratchett didn't write any fantasy tales during the 1970s. *The Carpet People* had been written in the late 1960s, and his next novel – his only novel from the 1970s – *The Dark Side of the Sun*, would be a stab at a science fiction novel. This second book would be written during the evenings and published by Colin Smythe in 1976, shortly after the birth of Pratchett's daughter Rhianna. The rest of the 1970s saw him continue his career in journalism and bring up his daughter, interspersed with intervals of serious gardening, one of Pratchett's favourite pastimes. His passion for writing was now the day job, and his priorities had to change slightly with a young family to provide for. So it is interesting, then, that as soon as he gave up journalism, he started writing novels with a passion.

'He says it gives the place a friendly and open aspect. Friendly and open aspect! I've seen keen gardeners break down and cry.'

(*Eric*)

CHAPTER THREE

And as if by Magic...

'Technically I'm a humanist. I don't believe in big
beards in the sky, but I do believe there is an order.'

Terry Pratchett

While Pink Floyd were content to take you only to 'The Dark
Side of the Moon', Pratchett took you to *The Dark Side of the
Sun*. OK, Pink Floyd didn't tell you which moon exactly, but
then again Pratchett didn't tell you which sun.

Although Pratchett had a love affair with the fantasy genre, he
also had a clear passion for science fiction too, and his second
novel *The Dark Side of the Sun* showcased that well. Although a
slim volume like all his early works (because he was in full-time
employment at the time), *The Dark Side of the Sun* turned as
many science fiction clichés on their heads as his first Discworld
novel would later do in the fantasy genre.★

Pratchett also drew the illustration for the dustwrapper of *The Dark Side of the Sun*.

In the 1960s Pratchett had been voraciously reading all the fantasy and science fiction he could and learning his trade as a journalist. By default he had become a writer of short fantasy stories, both at school and through the Uncle Jim column. Also, through Uncle Jim, the Carpet People had been born and the story tightened up for his first novel at the start of the 1970s. So there is a natural progression in Pratchett's work.

Five years would pass between the publication of *The Carpet People* (1971) and *The Dark Side of the Sun* (1976), but one must remember that Pratchett was a professional journalist with a young family and the books were only a hobby. They weren't generating serious money and wouldn't until approximately the publication of *Mort* (1987), just over 20 years after writing his Uncle Jim column, but Pratchett didn't expect them to.

The 1970s were a crucial part of the process that led to his Discworld books. *The Dark Side of the Sun* kept his hand in until he gave up journalism at the turn of the 1980s and he had time to write his second science fiction novel, *Strata*, which was – like *The Carpet People* – based on a discworld. But before we look at Pratchett's life after journalism, let us take a look at *The Dark Side of the Sun*, as it raises some important issues regarding the divide between fantasy and science fiction and, more importantly, where Pratchett sees that divide.

'The Editor stood up with a sigh. "What a pity it is you're not a writer of stories!" he said, putting his hand on the Time Traveller's shoulder.'

HG Wells (*The Time Machine*)

It is quite clear that fantasy and science fiction have their origins in different places, with different writers, clichés and expectations. The science fiction novel was an extension of the Industrial Revolution, when Victorians began to speculate about the advances of science from the imagination of their scientists and engineers and from discoveries in astronomy. It is a modern genre, as much as the air force is a modern arm of the military. You could go way back and say that the scientists of mediaeval times – the ones who became court physicians and were originally herbalists, druids, wizards and necromancers – were the fulcrum of science fiction/fantasy, and even of speculative fiction in its many forms, because couple all that with knights and romance and you get a fantasy base crying out for dragons and swashbuckling adventure. As Pratchett says: 'Throw a dragon in a story and everyone will call it fantasy' (witness *Guards! Guards!*). There's truth in this statement, but the earlier genres of gothic, macabre and dark romance – now sub-genres of the wider remit of horror – are more applicable to fantasy than science fiction.

Pratchett believes that science fiction is really a sub-genre of fantasy, but I disagree. One can see where perhaps one genre might split into two distinct genres – but two genres, not one below another. The 19th and 20th centuries constructed a distinct history for each genre, given depth by quality authors and the film industry. However, some Hollywood directors took their own interpretation of a genre and made it their own, thus creating a fractured genre through the film industry. There is no better example of this than the works of HP Lovecraft. In 1931 Lovecraft wrote a novella entitled *At the Mountains of Madness*. It concerned an expedition to the Antarctic, around the areas partially explored by Shackleton, Amundsen and Scott. Above some gigantic mountains is an ancient city buried beneath the ice. A team of scientists go in to explore it. They marvel at the ancient hieroglyphs and architecture, but as they venture deeper and deeper into the dark troglodyte city, an eerie tension is building all the time.

'And now, when Danforth and I saw the freshly
glistening and reflectively iridescent black slime which
clung thickly to those headless bodies and stank
obscenely with that new, unknown odour whose cause
only a diseased fancy could envisage – clung to those
bodies and sparkled less voluminously on a smooth part
of the accursedly resculptured wall in a series of
grouped dots – we understood the quality of cosmic
fear to its uttermost depths. It was not fear of those
four missing others – for all too well did we suspect
they would do no harm again. Poor devils!'

HP Lovecraft (*At the Mountains of Madness*)

The above quote could be from any one of the *Alien* movies. As
the reader, you know something is waiting in the darkness ahead
for the main characters and, sure enough, a creature of
unimaginable horror hurtles after the party and the whole thing
becomes a chase novel back to civilisation. Again *Alien*.

Although far from popular when first published, *At the
Mountains of Madness* strongly influenced the science fiction
genre and probably was the instigator of injecting true horror
into it as well. There is no question that the broad body of
Lovecraft's work was influenced by the world's first true horror
writer, Edgar Allan Poe, but which films benefited from
Lovecraft's take on science fiction? A clear example would be
The Thing from Another World (1951), which was remade by John
Carpenter as the special-effects movie *The Thing* (1982). One of
the important plot developments for this story was the gradual
knocking-off of the main characters. Thirteen become 12, who
then become 11, then ten, nine, eight… and there we see an
echo in the movie franchise of *Alien*. But it doesn't end there.
Lovecraft introduced an extra wonder by using extreme –
remote – locations on our own planet for his chilling settings.

This continued in the science fiction film world with the Arctic in *The Beast from 20,000 Fathoms* (1953), progressing to the Amazon in *The Creature from the Black Lagoon* (1954), and then on to the Himalayas in *The Abominable Snowman* (1957).

The knock-on effect of the popularity of these movies, each a milestone within the science fiction genre, shows how much cross-pollination the genre has picked up from horror – i.e. HP Lovecraft with a dash of Poe, maybe – a prime example being *The Quatermass Experiment* (1953). Classic writers in each genre will influence good practice within the movie industry, for example HG Wells in science fiction, Bram Stoker in horror and L Frank Baum in fantasy (*The Wizard of Oz* is so important to the cinematographic evolution of fantasy on celluloid). But as Terry Nation (creator of the Daleks) once said: 'When I used to go and see science fiction movies they used to have H certificates for Horror.' The original 1950s version of *The War of the Worlds* is a good example of this bastardisation of the genre.

So we understand the modern legacy of three fundamental genres in this book, but does Pratchett? No, he doesn't. He doesn't like the constraints of tight genres, because they restrict his imagination. For example, at the very start of *The Dark Side of the Sun*, he has the main character out fishing for Dagon.

'The region was putrid with the carcasses of decaying fish, and of other less describable things which I saw protruding from the nasty mud of the unending plain.'

HP Lovecraft (*Dagon*)

In using Dagon, Pratchett is acknowledging HP Lovecraft, one of the great masters of horror. Lovecraft wrote a short horror story called *Dagon*, and this is echoed at the start of Pratchett's science fiction novel. So here we have a mixture – not necessarily a confusion – of genres, because there should be no boundary to imagination. However, one should still be aware of what the genres are.

So is *The Dark Side of the Sun* Pratchett's vision of the science fiction genre? Indeed it is. It echoes his beliefs as to what science fiction is: a sub-genre of fantasy that includes some early horror fiction too. Remember, for Pratchett, *Dr Who* fits into the sub-genre of science fiction. So Pratchett's ability to blend major influences from science fiction, fantasy and horror – whether motivated by the history of cinema or not – is unashamed and seamless.

> 'Shortly Don heard a warm Cockney voice, "Don, my
> dear boy, are you there?"
> "Yes, Sir Isaac."
> The dragon shrilled relief.'
>
> **Robert A Heinlein (*Between Planets*)**

Robert A Heinlein was one of the greatest practitioners of science fiction. His novel *Stranger in a Strange Land* (1961) is one of the most important science fiction novels ever written, and was too far ahead of its time to be fully appreciated in the early 1960s. The above quote comes from an earlier Heinlein novel that actually used dragons (and something a little *too* upper class to be Cockney). This illustrates that most genre writers try to mix and match, but, as I stated earlier, the main influence on a book or film will be its driving – defining – genre: science fiction, horror or fantasy. *Between Planets* was exactly what it said on the tin: science fiction. Despite some genre cross-contamination, Pratchett's *The Dark Side of the Sun* is exactly the same and based upon his take on the genre.

'The Dagon fishermen under licence from the Board of
Widdershins rode out by the hundred when the big
bivalves rose up from the deep, to snatch the pearls of
nacreous pilac by the light of the moon.'

(*The Dark Side of the Sun*)

Halfway through *The Dark Side of the Sun*, the science fiction
purist is a little frustrated. There is no science embedded in the
fiction thus far; everything is pure fantasy. The great practitioners
of the genre – Heinlein, Asimov, Clarke, Herbert – all had some
science and often deep political problems (witness *Foundation*,
Dune, *Time for the Stars*, even *The War of the Worlds*), but
Pratchett's science fiction has its soul in the fantasy genre. The
upside to this is some beautiful writing: 'Dom saw the huntsman
on his black horse when he brushed through the wall of the
drive cabin like bracken... For a moment he looked at Dom,
who saw his eyes gleam momentarily like mirrors and a hand go
up protectively. Then the horse and rider were gone.'

Pratchett takes in the illusions of space travel and
improbability drives as abstractly as Douglas Adams in *The
Hitchhiker's Guide to the Galaxy*, but at least Adams questioned
life, the universe and everything and did his improbability
maths, eventually coming up with the answer to the ultimate
question of life, the universe and everything as 42! Perhaps
Pratchett's rocky relationship with maths makes him ignore
fiddly calculations and mind-blowing telephone numbers of
digits, which explain how old your twin brother will be if he has
travelled at the speed of light while you grew old over 50-odd
years (see Heinlein's *Time for the Stars*). Probably true, as Asimov,
Heinlein and Clarke all loved playing with maths.

What Pratchett does well is play with words, approaching the
mysteries of the universe from a completely different viewpoint.
He looks at the absurdities that actually exist in life and takes a

moment to talk about them. A good example of this in *The Dark Side of the Sun* is where the subject of horse racing is discussed: '... on Earth there was a creature called a horse. Long ago it was realised that if a number of these animals were raced over a set distance one must surely prove faster than the others, and from this there was...' Gambling!

Pratchett does not believe in God, but he believes in an order to the universe. He is intrigued by the absurdity of life and the creations of mankind – he is a humanist – but as he admits nowadays, he is getting a little disillusioned with mankind and his cruelty to his fellow creatures. This is detectable in *The Dark Side of the Sun*, just as it would be later in the Discworld series and books such as *Johnny and the Dead* and *Nation*.

'They stared into the screen. On maximum magnification it showed a pyramid tumbling deceptively slowly through space, flashing faintly as starlight caught its polished faces.'

(*The Dark Side of the Sun*)

The above scene could be from any episode of the original *Star Trek*, another hit 1960s science fiction show of Pratchett's acquaintance. It acts as both a parody and a tribute to genre fiction past. He would do this time and time again in the Discworld series to a lesser or greater extent.

Personally, I believe Pratchett sums up his belief in God (or, rather, lack of it), the wider universe and the 'quest' of mankind in one specific quote from *The Dark Side of the Sun*:

'Understanding is the first step towards control. We now understand probability.
If we control it every man will be a magician. Let us then hope that this will not come to pass. For our

universe is a fragile house of atoms, held together by
the weak mortar of cause and effect. One magician
would be two too many.'

Charles Sub-Lunar, Cry *Continuum*
(*The Dark Side of the Sun*)

Towards the end of *The Dark Side of the Sun*, Pratchett discusses
the omnipresence of God, and the possibility of man actually
finding Him. He then explains that if a 'Director of the
Universe' were actually found it would cause chaos on Earth,
because: 'He would have ceased to become a matter of
comforting Belief but a matter of fact.' Pratchett goes further
and explains that mankind 'can't live and *know* of such
greatness', and he makes a very good point here. Mankind's lust
for knowledge and power would destroy itself, because the
passion and panic of discovering God would cause a conflict
with all variations of religion preached around the planet. (A
good old conflict of interests, but who would come out on top?)

'Next to her the electric toad flopped and rustled in its
box; she wondered what it "ate"... Artificial flies, she
decided.'

Philip K Dick (*Do Androids Dream of Electric Sheep?*)

There are many controlling robots and sub-levels of robot in
The Dark Side of the Sun, and when one sees metallic insects, one
cannot but think of *Do Androids Dream of Electric Sheep?* The
questioning of one's beliefs displayed by Pratchett in his first
science fiction novel is not dissimilar to the paranoia and desires
and self-analysis displayed in Philip K Dick's novel. Not that I'm
suggesting that Pratchett copied the style in any way; what it
illustrates is Pratchett's ability to question the existence of a
supreme being and then discuss the consequences of being

confronted with Him, which was done so brilliantly by Arthur C Clarke in *Childhood's End* when faced by an alien race resembling the Devil.

'There was no mistake. The leathery wings, the little
horns, the barbed tail – all were there. The most terrible
of all legends had come to life, out of the unknown
past. Yet now it stood smiling, in ebon majesty, and with
a human child resting trustfully on either arm.'

Arthur C Clarke (*Childhood's End*)

There are some nice pieces within *The Dark Side of the Sun*, but its heart and soul are embedded too far in the fantasy genre for it to have substance as a great science fiction novel. What it *is* – and where it has importance – is an exercise in what the Discworld novels *won't* become. Pratchett doesn't seem comfortable with the constraints of the science fiction novel, and he discovered that through writing this book. There are Discworld moments, such as the first mention of Hogswatch, and one can detect a fantasy novel screaming to come out, but it would take another book for Pratchett to realise that science fiction was not his genre. That would come five years later, in the more complete *Strata* (1981).

Strata is an intriguing book for anyone wishing to analyse Pratchett's life and works, because a) it predicts Discworld more fully than *The Carpet People,* and b) it says a little about the thinly documented job he was doing at the time.

In 1980 Pratchett quit journalism and joined the Central Electricity Generating Board, becoming press officer for three (or four, according to Pratchett's friend Sam Farr) nuclear power stations. He has notoriously said that he would write a book about his experiences if he thought anyone would actually believe them. Indeed, there are rumours of a character he calls

Fred, who once tipped nuclear waste down the toilet and caused all sorts of problems until someone brave enough – or experienced enough – was found to clear out the plant's septic tank. If indeed this story is true – and it probably vindicates Pratchett's fears that no one would believe the truth if he told it – it could have repercussions in the public arena as to how safe our nuclear power stations are. Pratchett spent eight years in the job (until 1987), when he suddenly realised that he was making more money from his Discworld novels than as a press officer.

In an online talk with the author ('Book World', *The Washington Post*), Pratchett summarised his time at the Central Electricity Generating Board: 'Let us be clear that I was no nuclear physicist. I was a press officer for a whole slew of power stations, but it was the three nuclear sites that always got the public interest. I fear many things more than I do nuclear power, at least in the hands of the Western democracies. I was once berated by a citizen who was worried about the existence of a power plant some 30 miles from where he lived. He lived extremely close to an automobile tyre manufacturing company and I wondered if he would sleep safe in his bed if he knew all the chemicals that they used. This all segues into the global warming debate, but surely in essence it is quite simple. Either we really are Homo sapiens, in which case we should be able to think, talk and negotiate ourselves out of the problem, or we are simply still Pan narrans, the storytelling chimpanzee. It's time for us to use our big brains.'

So, with this in mind, let us now take a look at Pratchett's second – and final – science fiction novel. *Strata* was published in June 1981 in a print run of 3,001 copies: 2,000 copies being issued in the United States by St Martin's Press and 1,001 in Britain under the Colin Smythe imprint. Of these, 850 copies were sold to the Readers' Union, so the intentions for the book were modest.

Strata opens with a man and a woman being caught by their corporation for placing a plesiosaur in the wrong stratum holding a placard, which reads 'End Nuclear Testing Now'. Clearly, the new job was giving Pratchett some inspiration. But *Strata* is a more important novel than that. It is a book of discovery – for Pratchett. It's as though you are allowed to glimpse the Eureka moment of the creation of the Discworld series.

To begin with, *Strata* is influenced by the great NEL science fiction paperback onslaught of the 1970s and early 1980s. You can witness influences from Heinlein, Van Vogt and Clarke, to name but three, but then the book takes a sharp turn. A Discworld with 35,000-mile-long waterfalls around it, where the sea literally falls over the edges, a bar called the Broken Drum, a whimsical magic purse that makes one think of the walking Luggage (in the very next novel) – there are many comparisons to be made, but then everything suddenly falls into place. This is due to the arrival of the character called Sphandor, who speaks in capital letters, just like Death will throughout the Discworld series. When Sphandor arrives, the banter, the fun, the effortless sending characters on their merry way to risk life and limb to do their best (or worst) are there, almost completely out of the blue.

Strata is largely overlooked, and that's a great shame. Just as albums such as *The Man Who Sold the World* and *Born to Run* shaped the future of rock 'n' roll for Bowie and Springsteen, *Strata* shaped the future for Terry Pratchett and ultimately the fantasy genre. It is a science fiction novel that changes genres halfway through, which is an interesting concept.

I never find the use of swearing valid in a Terry Pratchett novel, as it conflicts with the delicacy of the humour. There is a little of it in *Strata* along with a little homage to the great comedian and iconoclast Spike Milligan. When one of the characters says 'We must handle this carefully', Kin Arad (the main character) replies 'I like the *we.*' This pays homage to the opening page of Spike's first war biography, *Adolf Hitler: My Part in His Downfall* – when the prime minister speaks on the radio and says: 'As from 11 o'clock today we are at war with Germany.' Spike replies: 'I loved the *WE.*'

One could say that Pratchett pushed the boundaries of the fantasy genre as much as Milligan did the comedy genre, and by using nothing more than imagination without constraint. They (Milligan and Pratchett) didn't listen to the words of convention; they made the whole thing up as they went along and found a loyal audience following their multicoloured inventions.

> 'We played "Highland Laddie"; at once the floor
> became a mass of leaping twits all yelling "Och! Aye!"
> This is where the fight started.'
> **Spike Milligan (*Adolf Hitler: My Part in His Downfall*)**

At his most inventive, Pratchett has an element of Milligan about him. The Nac Mac Feegle (*The Wee Free Men*) of the Tiffany Aching novels are a good example, and indeed Pratchett considers these books some of his very best in the Discworld series.

Great artists don't always get it right, but when they do it's nothing short of magical. Going back to the rock 'n' roll comparison, the same can be said of David Bowie. When he is on form, music such as 'Ashes to Ashes' and 'Heroes' is created; when he is poor, however, all sorts of nonsense like 'The Laughing Gnome' and 'Beat of the Drum' surfaces. But you learn to take the rough with the smooth: the downside is made up for by the thrill of the upside. The same could be said about one-time snooker genius Alex 'Hurricane' Higgins: one moment a near-impossible shot is achieved, the next complete meltdown.

So has Terry Pratchett released some bad books? Not necessarily, but like most writers he sometimes hasn't given his best, for whatever reason. Personally I don't rate *The Dark Side of the Sun*, but it was important for Pratchett to get science fiction out of his system. I'm also not a fan of *The Carpet People* – especially the new version (more about that later) – and the Night Watch are not my favourite characters either (although they are for a lot of people), but when somebody has released such a large body of work, different people have their own favourites. Fans rarely come in at the beginning of an author's career, and often the book that introduces them to a writer becomes their favourite. For Pratchett fans that can be books as diverse as *Johnny and the Bomb*, *The Wee Free Men* and *The Amazing Maurice and his Educated Rodents* rather than *The Colour of Magic*, *Mort* or *Eric* (more about those later too).

I believe that Pratchett knew where he would set the next novel after *Strata* – a discworld, even if he didn't know what it would be about. The evidence is in the timeline. In 1971 he released his first novel, in 1976 his next, then in 1981 his third – and in 1983 his fourth. The gap between the third and fourth books is very short. Couple that with the introduction of a discworld – not necessarily the discworld in *Strata* – and we witness a clear way forwards; you can detect the Eureka in the text. Hindsight is a marvellous thing, and being familiar with the Discworld books and then reading *Strata* provides the thrill of discovery.

One last point about *Strata* and its discworld: it is a machine, and like any all-powerful machine it is potentially dangerous. 'It looks like an explosion in a power station,' one character declares of the interior of the disc. Repairing the chaos is then considered, but it appears to be a forlorn hope as the disc-makers are long since dead. Then we have the most important line: '"Memes are – ideas, attitudes, concepts, techniques," said

Kin. "Mental genes. Trouble is, all the memes likely to develop on the disc are host-destructive..."' We witness the great machine controlling the world and I cannot put out of my mind the thought that Pratchett was effectively working for the nuclear industry at the time. Chernobyl and the Japanese earthquake were still in the future, but Pratchett had seen and heard much he clearly didn't like in his new job, but he would have to stick with it for a few more years yet.

So writing the books suddenly became a therapy. And after – or rather during – *Strata*, the Discworld was created and his next book would be *The Colour of Magic*.

'Moon Watcher came face to face with the New Rock when he led the tribe down to the river in the first light of morning... It was a rectangular slab, three times his height... it was not easy to see except when the rising sun glinted on its edges.'
Arthur C Clarke (*2001 – A Space Odyssey*)

Part Two
A Fantasy World

'There was once a child, and he strolled about a good deal, and thought of a number of things.'
Charles Dickens ('*A Child's Dream of a Star*')

CHAPTER FOUR

The Colour of Magic

'Being Ymor's right-hand man was like being gently
flogged to death with scented bootlaces.'

(The Colour of Magic)

Scientist Stephen Hawking started his book *A Brief History of
Time* with an anecdote reputedly from the mathematician and
philosopher Bertrand Russell, who in a lecture once described
how Earth orbited around the sun and how the sun, in turn,
orbited around the centre of a vast collection of stars called our
galaxy. At the end of the lecture, a little old lady got up and
argued that what he had just said was a load of rubbish and that
the world was really flat and supported on the back of a giant
tortoise – in fact the tortoise was supported by many other
tortoises all the way down to who knows where.

'Most people would find the picture of our universe as
an infinite tower of tortoises rather ridiculous, but why

do we think we know better? What do we know about
the universe, and how do we know it? Where did the
universe come from, and where is it going?'
Stephen Hawking (*A Brief History of Time*)

Pratchett's fourth novel, *The Colour of Magic*, would set the pace
for the next 30 years. It changed the direction of the writer's
work, the prologue shaping a brand new Narnia. The idea that a
flat – disc – world could be carried on the backs of four giant
elephants, which were in turn on the back of a giant interstellar
turtle (not a tortoise), took a different planet out of the comfort
zone of science fiction and placed it firmly in the Fantasy genre
with a large capital F.

Pratchett mixed the mediaeval western assumption that the
world was flat with the ancient Hindu mythology that elephants
and great turtles carried the world on their backs. He gave the
characters names: the turtle, Great A'Tuin, the elephants, Berilia,
Tubul, Great T'Phon and Jerakeen. But Pratchett didn't dwell on
these mystical creatures in his novel. Apart from the two main
characters, Rincewind and Twoflower (and Twoflower's Luggage
made of sapient pearwood), he didn't dwell on anyone or
anything too much. This is highlighted by the use of the gods
that live above the world and play games with the characters
who reside beneath. Although they emulate Zeus and his fellow
gods in the story of Jason and the Argonauts, the gods have very
little place or importance in the novel. They're just there to add
to the madness.

The Discworld is an enchanted land. It has gods who play
with the beings below them, it has wizards and witches,
barbarians and dragons, but it also has the ability to laugh at
itself. The fact that Pratchett calls a passing character Blind Hugh
(so close to Robert Louis Stevenson's Blind Pew from *Treasure
Island*) is enough to tell the reader that the author isn't taking

himself too seriously. The book moves at pace through imaginative scenes with a multitude of characters whose blink-and-you-miss-them presence gives the reader a real appetite to know more. There is very little plot, as imagination is the driving force, not unlike Dickens' *The Pickwick Papers*. Indeed, Pratchett calls *The Colour of Magic* a road movie before roads were invented, which means *The Pickwick Papers* was a road movie as soon as commercial transport *was* invented.

Pratchett has said that he didn't really know what he was doing at the time of conceiving and writing *The Colour of Magic* but he admits that he wrote it for himself, i.e. for somebody who had been reared on the fantasy genre.* The Discworld novels are multilayered and evocative, and that's why they have endured over 40 novels in nearly 30 years. Like *The Lord of the Rings*, Discworld has created its own history, laws and legends, adding colour and light into what was a fading genre, which now, partly to Pratchett's credit and influence (and partly thanks to JK Rowling), is on the rise again.

Pratchett has said that *The Colour of Magic* was written in protest against the fantasy boom of the 1970s where people were influenced by a whole host of writers who were inevitably influenced by JRR Tolkien. *The Silmarillion* was published in the late 1970s and Tolkien's presence is a heavy one, but I do think this is posthumous analysis, as Pratchett has admitted that he didn't know what he was doing at the time!

Pratchett considered the fantasy genre dead in the early 1980s. He thought it lacked imagination – the very thing that should fuel it – and that it was just regurgitating tried and proven scenarios. This was showcased very prominently in the second

---

I do challenge Pratchett's belief that he didn't know what he was doing. *Strata* became Discworld and Pratchett must have known what direction he was going to move into.

Discworld novel, *The Light Fantastic*. Within that book there is a very old character called Cohen the Barbarian, a send-up of an aged Conan the Barbarian from Robert E Howard's classic tales. The swordswoman Herrena reflects on the drawbacks of her career: men not taking her seriously until she has killed them and the heartache of the clichéd leather straps she wore that brought her out in a rash. Pratchett says that *all* the female barbarians are scantily clad in leather in fantasy novels, and of course he's right, demonstrating much laziness by fellow writers.

This is where we begin to understand more about *The Colour of Magic*. It was written after many years of avid reading of fantasy novels, of *knowing* that wizards were more powerful than witches – sexism is prevalent in fantasy – and everyone wearing the clothes of cliché. This is something Pratchett mentions at the end of *The Wee Free Men*, where the heroine has to allow a boy to take the credit for all the good she does in saving him and her baby brother from the Queen of Fairyland. In *The Colour of Magic*, Pratchett decided to tear down the clichés of fantasy and have as a hero a wizard who would be surprised if the magic he harboured actually worked. In too many fantasy novels a wizard would stretch out his fingers and somebody would be blown to bits, with the exception of Gandalf, whose powers are largely hidden in *The Lord of the Rings*.

Also, with the Discworld novels Pratchett decided to take chances with a genre that had gone stale and to mock it from the inside. What other writer, for example, would put a condom factory in his make-believe world? Not Tolkien or Lewis for sure – that would be well outside their comfort zone – but Pratchett hardly bats an eyelid when doing so later in the Discworld series.

It is all well and good to satirise a genre within an adventure, but there has to be something new to offer as well. For Pratchett and *The Colour of Magic* that was the colour of magic itself. Part of the real innovation of the book was the eighth colour of the Rimbow, octarine, which is caused 'by the scatter-effect of strong sunlight on an intense magical field'. Pratchett uses the colour to name a book, *The Octarine Fairy Book*, paying homage to Andrew Lang's series of coloured Fairy Books (see Further Reading).

So what does Pratchett say of *The Colour of Magic*? He says it is a fun book and the whole series has grown out of that steady foundation. But what made it a milestone in Pratchett's canon? What inspired another 40-odd books? Where did it come from? We have seen that the idea was a natural progression from his previous three novels; now let us understand a little about the story.

When we first meet Rincewind, 'a gutter wizard' who doesn't believe in his own magical powers, he is under the influence of a fear-quenching drug. His laid-back attitude when confronted by two robbers is offhand, even though he admits to being terrified. It is this lack of concern about impending danger that reminds the reader of Zaphod Beeblebrox from Douglas Adams' *The Hitchhiker's Guide to the Galaxy*, who had special glasses that went black when danger approached. Rincewind's drug has the same useless power, heightening his fear threshold to a useless level.

The absurd/sublime humour of Pratchett is not dissimilar to that of Adams. Indeed, both authors were writing their respective series of books at the same time, and one could justifiably sum up the humour of the day – the early 1980s – with these two different works. That humour was also present in BBC TVs *Doctor Who* at that time, especially in leading actor Tom Baker, as Adams was the scriptwriter of the show in the early 1980s.

Where *The Hitchhiker's Guide to the Galaxy* has a tour guide in Ford Prefect, *The Colour of Magic* has a tourist called Twoflower.

Like millions of real-life tourists the world over, Twoflower is always losing his luggage, but unlike real-life tourists, his luggage sprouts legs and follows him wherever he goes.

There is also something endearing about Twoflower. He is oblivious to the danger around him because he believes that, as a tourist, nothing can really hurt him. This is always the catalyst for chaos. Rincewind, who finds himself stuck with the irritating fellow, is exasperated by him but fails to see that he is as much to blame. In this respect Rincewind and Twoflower are not unlike Laurel and Hardy, trapped in the chaos of their own innocence. Indeed, Pratchett pays tribute to the comic geniuses when Rincewind coins one of Oliver Hardy's most famous lines: 'Here's another fine mess you've got me into.'

Pratchett says of his characters: 'Twoflower was a joke. The archetypal tourist… And Rincewind is there to protect him. Rincewind's tragedy is he thinks magic shouldn't work.'

'Rincewind… was expecting to boldly go where no man – other than the occasional luckless sailor, who didn't really count – had boldly gone before…'

(*The Colour of Magic*)

Pratchett plays with cult one-liners. Some the audience will pick up on, others they won't. At the end of *The Wee Free Men*, a witch says 'Come sisters, we must away,' whereupon she is chastised for coming out with such 'theatre talk'. As there are three witches, one instantly thinks of the Scottish play in Shakespeare's canon. The point is: all of these comparisons and one-liners are there if you want them. If you simply wish to have a technicolour fantasy adventure story, you've got that too, but parody is never far from Pratchett's heart.

Let us now move on a little and look at the geography of Discworld. Early in *The Colour of Magic* we see the Ankh River that transports ships to the city of Ankh-Morpork. The river is known to burst its banks on occasion, so there we have a comparison with, or rather a suggestion of, Egypt and the Nile River, without any additional reason than a visual image and perhaps the Ankh symbol so often associated with Egypt and the pharaoh Tutankhamun.

Discworld is an intriguing blend of various scenes from times past. There is the Egyptian theme with its multitude of gods. There is the first description of Ankh-Morpork, which is akin to a Chicago-style gangsters' den straight out of the 1930s. And then there is the brawl Rincewind witnesses when first visiting a bar (Wild West maybe?), where he is nearly hit by a flying axe resembling a partridge (suddenly ancient Viking battles seem to be the order of the day). Ankh-Morpork is a blend of different histories that shape-shift from house to house. Perhaps it is this never-ending line of images that has fed Pratchett's imagination and constantly beckoned him to return to the series, but that is the kind of thing great fantasies are made of. The Discworld is whatever its creator wants it to be. It can be highly moral, judgemental and socially aware, or just plain fantasy, and it is this unpredictability – along with its humour – that has kept the series fresh and engaging.

Readers all over the world identify with Ankh-Morpork. 'It's probably my greatest success in *The Colour of Magic*,' Pratchett says, and he's probably right. Readers believe that it is based on Venice, Prague, New York, London… the list goes on – wherever they live, Ankh-Morpork is their home. It's vibrant from the off, original in its ability to be unoriginal. It vindicates Pratchett's whimsical aside that *The Colour of Magic* was intended to do as much for the fantasy genre as *Blazing Saddles* did for the Western: it pokes fun at its genre and teases the reader too, moving too quickly to make any bold or lasting statement.

The Colour of Magic is similarly a fast-paced novel, and because of that one could say that it is a chase novel or high adventure novel. Throughout the book Death rears his head, talking in CAPITAL LETTERS without speech marks. 'I introduced Death for a gag,' Pratchett says, 'where people flee to escape death. But of course no one can and he expected to meet you there [wherever you are] anyway.' The latter part of the quote is quite right, but I do disagree with the former part, because Death had already been introduced with a very short cameo role in *Strata*. But the point is that life and death are two intriguing concepts in Pratchett's novels, and thus a strong part of the force that makes him want to keep writing.

At the beginning of the Discworld series, Rincewind was the perfect character through which Pratchett could explore some of the antics of Death. Because Rincewind is a wizard, he is entitled to have Death present at his own death; Death keeps turning up but Rincewind still keeps escaping the great inevitable. In fact, as Rincewind declares, he's seen his life flash in front of his eyes so often he now falls asleep during the boring bits. But as with everyone, death – or Death – catches up with him eventually, but not in *The Colour of Magic*.

'... the Discworld has only one possible saviour.
Unfortunately, this happens to be the singularly inept
and cowardly wizard called Rincewind, who was last
seen falling off the edge of the world...'

(Jacket blurb, *The Light Fantastic*)

There are books about the science of Discworld but what is interesting is the correlation between science and magic. Back in the 1970s there was a popular TV programme for children entitled *Catweazle*. The show was based around a magician from the Middle Ages who is propelled into the 1970s and is amazed by the magic all around him. The telephone is 'the telling-bone', electricity is 'elec-trickery', and this sums up Pratchett's views on science and magic. In conversation he recalls GK Chesterton, who said in one of his essays that a streetlight is more interesting than magic. By this he meant that the process that went into making the light bulb – monkeys into humans, tungsten inside a glass bulb – or the chain of events that made it is 'more wildly magical than the concept of magic' and he's probably right.

Life is far less commonplace than we admit. Human beings always make the observation that if you wrote real events as fiction you wouldn't be believed, and there is so much truth in that. As Sir Arthur Conan Doyle famously wrote in 'A Case of Identity' (*The Adventures of Sherlock Holmes*): '"My dear fellow," said Sherlock Holmes... "life is infinitely stranger than anything which the mind of man could invent... if we could fly out of that window hand in hand, hover over this great city, gently remove the roofs, and peep in at the queer things which are going on, the strange coincidences, the plannings, the cross-purposes, the wonderful chain of events, working through generations... it would make all fiction... most stale and unprofitable."'

'Everybody should be allowed to blow up their own pub,' Pratchett says. Indeed the irreverent humour of the author, along with his cutting-edge originality, has given the fantasy genre a new start. He really did blow up his own pub – the fantasy genre as we knew it – and started afresh. Although Douglas Adams' work carved a whole new niche in the science fiction genre, one can see the influence of Pratchett in great fantasies since the beginning of the Discworld series, from JK Rowling to Jasper Fforde. Indeed, Pratchett says of Fforde: '[He is] ingenious – I'll watch Jasper Fforde nervously.' One could say that the endorsement is kindly, but when reviewers suddenly compare Fforde to Douglas Adams as well, one can see the thick blanket of humour that Pratchett and Adams draped over the whole science fiction/fantasy bandwagon influencing and encouraging a whole new generation of writers and artists from the early 1980s to at least the end of the millennium.

'Urban vampires were once more heavily forecast for the week ahead, with scattered wizards moving in from Wednesday and a high chance of Daphne Farquitt novels near the end of the week.'

Jasper Fforde (*One of Our Thursdays is Missing*)

The whimsical, irreverent style in Fforde's work is evocative of classic Adams and Pratchett. This isn't a criticism of Fforde, it's a compliment, as both Adams and Pratchett reminded aspiring writers that it was OK to take chances in creative writing, to dare to be different and, most of all, to break down the establishment of genre fiction, which both Pratchett and Fforde have really made their own territory today.

Let us now analyse this great awakening as far as Pratchett was concerned. Was *The Colour of Magic* an overnight success? No, it wasn't. It couldn't be, the print run was too low for one thing.

The Colour of Magic was published by Colin Smythe in November 1983 and has since become one of the most collectable Pratchett books you are likely to find. The print run was 4,540 copies, 506 coming from St Martin's Press in the United States. This means that, contrary to common belief, it was *not* a bestseller in its original hardback.

The first UK edition was bound in light green cloth boards with gilt lettering, making it most attractive. Alan Smith created the striking colour dustwrapper, featuring the turtle, elephants and Discworld moving through space. The original UK dustwrapper carried no price but the first issue had a price sticker of £7.95 in the UK and $11.95 in the US. The jackets were otherwise identical, but the collector should note that there is a huge difference in price nowadays: approximately £4,000 for a UK copy compared with £200 for a US counterpart.

Just to confuse people, later issues of the UK version included US reviews on the inside flap of the jacket to cover the original blurb, which contained a mistake. Whoever had written it had called Twoflower an intergalactic tourist, which of course he was not.

The American Science Fiction Book Club issued a copy in 1994. Collectors can tell the difference between the two US editions by the length of the book – 184 pages in the Science Fiction Book Club edition as opposed to the 206 pages of the first edition – and, of course, the words 'Book Club Edition' on the front inner flap of the dustwrapper. Colin Smythe imported 400 copies of this edition, selling them with a UK price sticker. Corgi published the first paperback edition in 1985, Smythe having cleared the option rights with NEL, who later regretted it.

All of this information also shows the small moves the Discworld series made in its early days. For example, it wasn't until the Corgi paperback that Pratchett decided to bring back Rincewind in *The Light Fantastic* (1986), a seamless sequel to *The Colour of Magic*, but one with more plot – and consequently less spontaneous imagery – than its predecessor (although Pratchett would argue that the first four novels were plotless).

Anyone interested in collecting Terry Pratchett wants all these early editions because they are the proof – the blueprint – of the unfolding evolution of the Discworld series. If *The Colour of Magic* hadn't sold well in paperback, we probably wouldn't have had further novels in the series. But why did it sell well in paperback? Word of mouth or more copies printed? In fact, it was due to the BBC serialising the novel in six parts on their radio show *Woman's Hour*. It was directly after this happened that sales took off.

The Light Fantastic was a good commercial move. Continuing the story of Rincewind and the multicoloured chaos of the Discworld, it was a more important book than its predecessor if only because, a year after its release, Pratchett had made enough money to give up the day job and become a full-time writer. He welcomed the move with open arms, digging deeper into the fantasy world of Discworld, creating new and more outrageous characters, and amassing a legion of fans. He had now hit on the winning formula, but as we have seen, that formula had been building since his school days.

It is worth mentioning that a joint publication by Smythe and Gollancz didn't work, but Pratchett considered Smythe a friend so he asked him to be his agent instead. Smythe agreed and it became a sound partnership from then on.

'We find ourselves in a bewildering world. We want to make sense of what we see around us and to ask: what is the nature of the universe? What is our place in it and where did it and we come from?'

Stephen Hawking (*A Brief History of Time*)

CHAPTER FIVE

Tripping the Light Fandango

'... if a poet sees a daffodil he stares at it and writes a long poem about it, but Twoflower wanders off to find a book on botany. And treads on it... He just looks at things, but nothing he looks at is ever the same again. Including me...'

(Rincewind in *The Light Fantastic*)

The Light Fantastic slowed Rincewind down and made him take stock of who he was and what powers he truly had. There was a tenuous story too: the Discworld is on a collision course with a red star and only the secret spell somewhere in Rincewind's head can stop the catastrophe. All hell breaks loose until Rincewind can expel the spell.

Although we begin to understand Rincewind more in *The Light Fantastic* and appreciate the satirical edge of the Discworld mindset, the story is less satisfying than its predecessor. *The Colour of Magic* succeeded because it was pure fantasy that surged towards its final page like a branch between the shoulders of a mighty river; it was breathtaking and splendid in its visual plight. It won an audience and *The Light Fantastic* kept that story going. Although the format – and characters – changed thereafter, the Discworld had attracted an audience that would grow and grow from then on, but Twoflower and Rincewind grew apart in *The Light Fantastic.*

Rincewind says that whatever Twoflower looked at was never the same again, and unfortunately that echoes the mania of so many tourists in the world today. The Great Pyramid in Egypt, the other tombs and temples of that great land, even the prized and well protected treasures of Tutankhamun, have depreciated because of the damage caused by the insatiable tourist over the past hundred years (even though the monuments are thousands of years old). A Native American once said: when you visit us, take nothing but memories and leave nothing but footprints. Nothing could be more apt, but nothing could be further from Twoflower's thoughts.

Unlike the Fellowship, who embrace the friendship of talking trees in *The Lord of the Rings,* Rincewind doesn't reciprocate even when they talk to him. He clearly had heard the Goons song 'I talk to the trees, that's why they put me away'. People were beginning to love Pratchett's sense of humour; his back catalogue had started to sell out and he decided that a third Discworld novel would be a lucrative idea. *Equal Rites* would be that third novel and prove to be the first real departure for the series. About 100 proof copies were made up for writers and reviewers and suddenly the public was beginning to await the next episode in the Discworld saga. The money wasn't yet a flood, but the books' popularity was growing significantly.

Rincewind, Twoflower and Luggage made Pratchett famous. They set the scene for Discworld, but soon afterwards – several books in – they were put to one side so more characters could be introduced, from witches and more wizards to city guards. But for me there was something deeply magical about the early books; let us generalise and say that Rincewind was the character who became the Raphael-interpreted Doubting Thomas of the whole fantasy genre. He broke the mould and made a multitude of fans wake up and say, that's right, the genre shouldn't be so stereotypical. Rincewind was the cynical Pratchett within the novel, attacking such sacred cows as Conan the Barbarian and any other stereotype that came his way. But the series had to evolve. More characters and situations were needed. Clearly Pratchett was aware that he had hit a winning formula with the Discworld series.

Equal Rites is probably the most important book as far as giving breadth to the series is concerned. It is the first in which Granny Weatherwax appears and it concerns itself with an extension of the breaking down of fantasy clichés that was begun by *The Colour of Magic*. Instead of magic being passed down to the seventh son of the seventh son, we have the eighth son of the eighth son – eight being a very magical number in the series. But a calamity strikes: the eighth son happens to be a girl. At the moment of his death, the wizard Drum Billet passes on the wizard's staff and magic to a girl by mistake; whoever heard of a girl wizard? A witch maybe, but not a wizard. And there starts the genre-breaking story of female wizard Eskarina (Esk) Smith.

For me, *Equal Rites* is the very best book in the Discworld series. By this book Pratchett has homed in on the sexism of the whole fantasy genre, with witches having lesser powers than wizards and it being accepted as fact that females are only good for flying on broomsticks and throwing eye of newt into a bubbling cauldron. It was brave and ingenious and delivered different characters and places on the Discworld. The tempo was different too. It started from a fixed location and moved slowly forwards from there. With the characters not surrounded by chaos, Pratchett could delve a little more thoroughly into areas of the fantasy genre that intrigued him. He asks: what is magic? Then he explains that creating magic gives the witches and wizards nightmares and, from there, he buries himself in an interesting piece of speculation between Esk and Granny Weatherwax. They talk about the ability to perform magic, how to harness it, to control it. This is a very important part of the story and, ostensibly, the creation of the whole magical world in the Discworld series. It's a very long conversation that lasts several pages, but starts quite simply with Granny Weatherwax asking Esk what she wants to do when she grows up (a question that crops up from time to time in Pratchett's novels).

Like every other child, Esk doesn't know the answer, but unfortunately the realities of life have to be faced from the onset of one's teenage years, and Esk is no exception to this. Does she want to grow up or does she want to become a witch? That – for Esk – is the choice, making the decision to go into the profession of a witch akin to that of going into the priesthood. Pratchett confirms this with the line: '… they [witches] were respected… for doing a job which logically had to be done, but people never felt quite comfortable in the same room with them.'

Esk approaches the whole concept of being a witch – or wizard – with wide-eyed naivety and Granny Weatherwax has to deal with that, not unlike any form teacher in a modern-day secondary school when discussing students' future careers.

There is something very different about the first four novels in the Discworld series. They paint a huge and varied picture. They embrace a cornucopia of ideas. They only occasionally linger to build characters or to instruct in the sacred art of magic. They were a multicoloured blur that encapsulated the very best of the fantasy genre's fun and imagination at that time. They lacked parameters, which lesser Discworld titles, such as *A Hat Full of Sky*, had in abundance. Some could say that Pratchett has refined his style over the years, and although this could be true for novels such as *Going Postal* and *Making Money*, I do think it has been an albatross around the neck of some other books in the series.

All writers slow down a little, and although they may consider their later work to be their best, the fans normally go for the earlier novels, and not just for nostalgia's sake. Some of the early ideas are ingenious and important to the overall mindset, none more telling than the long conversation Granny Weatherwax has with Esk in the first quarter of *Equal Rites*. The conversation explores the meaning of magic in the real world. It argues that the core of magic has its basis in worldly knowledge, e.g. to the naïve the most basic things are magical. Adults invariably do something 'magical' to impress children. A good example of this is the bottle of sugary pink 'medicine' a doctor may prescribe a child when there is little wrong with them. It reassures both parent and child without offending. Incredibly, the child feels better soon afterwards. This is not a wild analogy on my part, because in Granny Weatherwax's conversation with Esk, she says that she saved a dying man by giving him a potion she told him was handed down to her from dwarves and had magical healing properties. In fact it was nothing of the kind, but the power of suggestion was enough to make the man recover – a rare magic indeed. So Pratchett is telling us that magic is around us in everyday life – it just needs to be used in the right way.

Esk is a fast learner, so much so that Granny Weatherwax allows her a small piece of magic in transferring part of her mind into an eagle, to feel what it can feel and see what it can see. However, Esk pushes things too far and her whole mind is consumed in the tiniest recess of the eagle's head and Granny has to force Esk back from the point of total absorption. This is a very interesting concept because it is something Pratchett returns to, but in a reverse way, in *A Hat Full of Sky*. In this instance a young witch – not unlike Esk – called Tiffany Aching leaves her body, only for it to be inhabited by a Hiver (a dangerous entity). This time it is the smallest part of Tiffany's brain that holds the former witch while the Hiver has control.

What I find refreshing about these 'possessions' is the scientific, rather than horrific, way in which they are tackled. There are no priests performing stomach-churning exorcisms, just everyday witches (sic) earning a crust to free the host.

Although the possession of Esk's body takes place before she becomes a wizard – and her friend is predictably cured of a stutter – there is satisfaction in the final pay-off to the novel because it dared to break down the fantasy myth that all wizards must be men. Women can be wizards too and, if the Discworld series had concluded as a trilogy, I would venture that the three books would still be incredibly important as genre-challenging (and building) stories by a man who was browned off with the repetition of cliché. To me, the first page of *Equal Rites* alone wins an award for daring to tread where no man – or woman – had trodden before.* Like the first two novels in the series, *Equal Rites* points a finger at the greats, such as the work of Robert E Howard and quite possibly *Doctor Who* as well, describing the Unseen University as 'bigger inside than out', surely a nod towards the Tardis. If we like our great novels in small packages tied with string, then perhaps Pratchett should have ceased writing the Discworld after *Equal Rites*, because it would have provoked more critique and would possibly have lent more greatness to the series.

Equal Rites was also read on the radio, which helped to increase the series' popularity.

'... it is primarily a story about a world. Here it comes
now. Watch closely, the special effects are quite
expensive.'

(*Equal Rites*)

At the end of *Equal Rites* we return to the wizard who started
all the problems, Drum Billet, who is reincarnated as an ant.
Along with his fellow ants, he inscribes a wall of a sugar pyramid
with the true secret of longevity, only to have it washed away the
very next time the Unseen University floods.★

Equal Rites is a novel about mistakes and pretence, a perfect
homage to the real world of politics and sycophancy.

Pratchett created the Unseen University as a satire on the Invisible College, which
was a collection of 17th-century scientists and philosophers, such as Robert Boyle,
John Evelyn, Francis Glisson, Robert Hooke, William Petty and Christopher Wren. In
some of his letters, Boyle refers to 'our invisible college' and 'our philosophical
college'. The basic thread throughout the group's activities was to use imagination
in their experimental endeavours.

CHAPTER SIX

Mort, Faust and Death

'Godless people might get up to anything, they might
turn against the fine old traditions of thrift and non-
self-sacrifice that had made the kingdom what it is
today...'

(*Eric*)

People don't change much during life. If we look at the
subjects that Pratchett selected for his A levels, we can see
where his interests and talents lay. He then used them well. He
completed his A level in English after leaving school, which
stood him in good stead for the *Bucks Free Press* and onwards
in his writing career. He kept his hand in with art, illustrating
The Carpet People and taking on other freelance work. Then
there is his interest in history, which he has drawn on in his
novels, two early examples in the Discworld series being
Pyramids and *Eric*.

'"We did it at school, the wooden horse, everything!"'

(Eric)

And at the same time there's that sense of humour, from the corny:

'"There's a door," he whispered.
"Where does it go?"
"It stays where it is, I think," said Rincewind.'

(Eric)

to the hysterical:

'"Come on. Let's run away."
"Where to?"
... "Don't worry about to," he said. "In my experience that always takes care of itself. The important word is away."'

(Eric)

Let us progress to *Eric* (1990), the ninth Discworld novel, as it is an interesting play on the 16th-century German legend of Faust.

Faustus means 'auspicious' or 'lucky' in Latin, so it's no surprise that when Eric, a 14-year-old counterpart to the ancient scholar, calls up a demon to give him worldly pleasures he gets Rincewind, the luckiest wizard on the Disc. Rincewind escapes the catacombs of the netherworld and Death once more, and of course Luggage follows, along with another strong dose of chaos and derring-do.

For long-term readers of the Discworld series, this fourth outing for the wizard is a welcome treat, and a departure from the growing number of witches appearing in the series. For me, Rincewind was the perfect guide to the Discworld. The spontaneity summoned up by the character creates an anarchy of the fantasy genre – i.e. a happy return to the reason why the Discworld was created in the first place. Any time Rincewind finds himself in a story, there is a comfortable flow like an ice-skating gold medalist finding perfect form again. So we return to a recurring Pratchett theme: God, creation, and the end of time. At the click of two fingers, Rincewind and Eric find themselves in utter darkness at the end of forever, and it is here that Pratchett queries the Big Bang theory, the 'gentle methods of Continuous Creation' and the shape of 'matter' (which includes the physical manifestation of old Kate Bush records!).

Discworld stories that jump around a lot, such as *The Colour of Magic* and *Eric,* have a thread in as much as they find an ultimate conclusion, proof that the chaos they have endured had a meaning, because the chaos somehow changed things for the better. It suggests that there is an order to the universe and if we truly understood it, there would be less chaos in our own lives. But if we did understand it, there would be a big upheaval in religious belief – because the existence of God would be proved.

Despite the never-ending string of gods in the Discworld series, Pratchett never rams down our throats his belief that God doesn't exist. Instead he speculates about the what ifs and what elses if not God? When Rincewind and Eric witness the birth of the universe, they don't meet *the* creator, they meet *a* creator, one of many beings that contributed to creation.

Pratchett doesn't believe that humans have got all the God stuff right. He gently lets you into his perception, emanating the moral teaching of the children's nursery story of 'The Sun and the Wind' (the wind blows fiercely to get what it wants, while the sun shines down its warming rays gently to coax the uninitiated). Although Pratchett's beliefs about religion are a major part of his life, he doesn't tarnish his stories with scathing comments; his sense of humour counters any chance of that.

There are lovely pieces in *Mort* (the fourth Discworld novel) that discuss human life. Questions such as: Why do humans put cherries on sticks and put them in drinks? Why do humans go to the lengths of putting their food in pastry before cooking it – surely life's too short? Why does the sun come out during the day? Why do teeth fit together so perfectly? All of these questions show an ability to stand back and look at the absurdity of the universe – our own personal universe, our own lives. It's the same mentality that made David Tennant's Doctor Who shake his head with a big broad grin and lovingly say 'humans', when seeing us enjoy the self-inflicted complications of our everyday lives. There is nothing derogatory in all of this. Pratchett isn't providing any answers – he's just stating that there is more going on in this wide universe than we credit, mainly because we largely take things for granted and complicate the detail.

As a species we complicate our lives with niff-naff and trivia – so much so that we don't see the lowly boy (Mort) walking across the floor at a party because our superior – adult – minds ignore him. From this we observe that the children in Pratchett's world hold the real magic. They make the changes; they apply a new logic that adults don't see. Tiffany Aching does very little magic; she applies logic and a cool head to her adventures and somehow gets through. Esk breaks down the traditions of the Unseen University to become the first female wizard. And what about Eric himself, the Discworld's very own Faust? He is a 14-year-old boy who longs for love and adventure and goes to great lengths to achieve them.

The impetuosity of youth? Of course, it's what feeds the human race. Without the burning ambitions of youth coupled with the experience of tradesmen (Death and his apprentice Mort), progress would be much slower. But these youthful characters aren't performing magic – they are creating a form of it by playing in their room, having to grow up and do their chores, by facing danger with no one defending their corner, and that is a harsh reality for many children around the world. Pratchett's advice to the younger readers is: make your own magic and question what is all around you. Curiosity is the trigger that allows you to find out about things. And that's great advice to give. Don't forget that the person who can argue that the works of Terry Pratchett are greater than the works of Charles Dickens is likely to get a degree in literature, not because they're right, but because they have put up a convincing argument that raises points that have a validity and have not been shared before. Questioning sacred cows, looking at things sideways, is what is important here, otherwise there can't be significant progress.

OLIVER TWIST AND MORT

The Sorcerer and the Apprentice is an age-old theme and one that can be exploited to either comic or sinister effect. In *Mort* we witness a young lad whose father puts him up for an apprenticeship but the only person who wants him is Death. Death tutors the boy in his ways of showing a lack of compassion when dealing with the nuances of the great inevitable. Life and death come to all, and Mort is taught harsh lessons, not unlike the young Oliver Twist by his own sorcerer Fagin.

Like Death, Fagin is both tutor and corruptor. Mort shouldn't really need a job helping souls on their way. He should live as a happy young apprentice in a world of young, like-minded people, but the young people he is in contact with – such as

Death's adopted daughter – are corrupted, or at least damaged due the influence of Death. This is also the dilemma of young Oliver Twist. He may be tutored by Fagin but it is the children he lives with who turn his mind to do wrong and believe it to be good and right. Like Dickens, Pratchett peoples his world with corrupted adults and, broadly speaking, innocent children placed in danger. The children are always victims of their circumstances, which mirrors the unpredictable world we all live in. There are always layers of evil, from the incredibly dangerous (Bill Sikes as Lilith) to the more cunning and manipulative (Fagin as Lord Vetinari). There are always guardian angels (Nancy as the Nac Mac Feegle). Although some children die, the majority are saved, thus leaving us with a more optimistic view of the world.

It is not in just the extreme situations in Oliver's story where we can draw a comparison – it is also in the more subtle scenes. Like Mort, Oliver enters into an apprenticeship and, like Mort, Oliver serves Death (in an undertaker's). Oliver struggles while serving his apprenticeship, as does Mort, but that's the reality of learning a trade in the real world.

'He was alone in a strange place; and we all know how chilled and desolate the best of us will sometimes feel in such a situation. The boy had no friends to care for, or to care for him. The regret of no recent separation was fresh in his mind; the absence of no loved and well-remembered face sank heavily into his heart. But his heart was heavy, notwithstanding; and he wished, as he crept into his narrow bed, that that were his coffin, and that he could be lain in a calm and lasting sleep in the church-yard ground, with the tall grass waving gently above his head, and the sound of the old bell to soothe him in his sleep.'

Charles Dickens (*Oliver Twist*)

Mort is older than Oliver. He is ready to go out into the world, and it's that level of maturity that saves Mort from despairing at his situation. However, when he begins to be conditioned by Death, he does try to escape the confines of the house of Death and seek living, breathing people. He falls in love with a queen, but a young queen who should be dead. He was there to take her soul but instead he saves her. So by the laws of nature she is dead but in reality she still breathes. Mort's unrequited love for the queen is a terrible weight to carry. He daren't tell Death that he has messed up, but Death is suddenly interested in mortality. As he drinks, dances and desperately tries to understand what makes humans drunk and be happy, Mort takes on the supernatural powers of his master – Death himself – and that's where a transformation begins to take place.

Pratchett's Death is not an unsavoury character – melancholy yes, but not hostile and scary. In a way, he could be described as uplifting. He talks conversationally about the one thing we all want to avoid discussing, thus stripping down the taboo and moving on to a more philosophical level (a little like Pratchett discussing assisted death).

Death's showcase book is *Reaper Man*. Although he may have a bit of a mid-life crisis in *Eric,* he's back to his age-old tricks a couple of books later, and there's something quite reassuring about that. The predictability of the world is a calming thing. It keeps the vast majority of humans sane, just as the omnipresence of God does. Faith in God is a major part of many people's lives. They draw strength from it, use it as a guiding light – a parameter – to structure and shape their family life. In many neighbourhoods faith also brings a community together, to share both good and bad experiences, to make sense of their collective and individual journey, to tackle the hard – terrible – moments and share the good times.

There are different types of faith and different types of belief.

We know Pratchett is not a believer in God, but he populates his imagination with many gods (plural) and other 'makers' (sometimes the human race; witness his science fiction novels). This is a constant theme.

> "'... I imagine there'll be some gods along soon. They don't wait long to move in... They tend to be a bit high-spirited to start with, but they soon settle down...'"
>
> (*Eric*)

Let us return to Mort for a while. Like Esk, like Eric, like Tiffany Aching, Mort reaches a crossroads in his life and has to make a decision about whether his choice in career is the right one. He has had a journey of self-discovery and has decided that the queen wasn't what he was truly looking for, but he did find a direction he wanted to take. And there's the crux of Pratchett's recurring theme. It's not just the self-discovery, it's the ability to drive it forwards from there – something that was so present in his own life during his teenage years. We will discuss Tiffany Aching in this context in a later chapter, and we will discover the theme again with Mau (in *Nation*), but what drives Mort? It is not faith in a superior being in the heavens above, it is being aware of his own mortality and understanding that he doesn't have the whole of eternity to get life right – he has one opportunity and the time to make it happen is now. And while it is unfair, the teenage years are exactly the right time to push children into thinking about their future life, and this is the right time on the Discworld too – or in the parallel world of *Nation* – to make things happen, because that's when there is the most enthusiasm for bettering oneself and still a smattering of wide-eyed wonder at the world around them.

There are many Terry Pratchett books that capture this key

theme and open a whole new multi-universe of opportunity for his younger fans, as great novels past have done in their way.

'Master Charles Bates, appalled by Sikes' crime, fell into a train of reflection whether an honest life was not, after all, the best. Arriving at the conclusion that it certainly was, he turned his back upon the scenes of the past, resolved to amend it in some new sphere of action. He struggled hard and suffered much, for some time; but having a contented disposition, and a good purpose, succeeded in the end; and, from being a farmer's drudge, and a carrier's lad, he is now the merriest young grazier in all Northamptonshire.'

Charles Dickens (*Oliver Twist*)

The Carpet People (again)

'History isn't something you live. It is something you
make. One decision. One person. At the right time.
Nothing is too small to make a difference. Anything can
be changed.'

(*The Carpet People*)

With the success of the Discworld series, around the time of
Mort, people started to get interested in Pratchett's early work.
The Carpet People was long out of print and the consensus of
opinion was that there was no demand for it. But there was.
Pratchett's fan-base grew and grew. First there was the little
'cult' following, and then there was a much larger Discworld
group that wanted to read the books that came before *The
Colour of Magic*.

The paperback of *The Colour of Magic* became extremely
successful, as had *The Light Fantastic* and the ten novels that
followed in the series, which really built an impressive following.

These books started the sort of obsessive fandom not uncommon in the science fiction and fantasy genres, and pressure to reprint Pratchett's early work became intense.

It was obvious that *The Carpet People* would sell well if reissued, but Pratchett wasn't content with it. He had written it when he was 17 years of age and in the traditional fantasy mindset that he was now so against in his early forties. So he decided that the book should be written by two people – the young Terry Pratchett and the older Terry Pratchett. He would revise and update it to fall more in line with the type of work he was doing with Discworld, i.e. breaking down the fantasy genre. He admitted that his older self wouldn't even think about writing such a book from scratch any more, but this was where his worlds would collide and *The Carpet People* was recast for posterity.

Was it a better book? Was it radically different? When horror writer James Herbert was approached to reissue *The Fog* in the mid-1980s, he mentioned in the special foreword that it would be wrong to rewrite the book, as if the tampering would in some way take away the energy of the book. As we have seen, cult writer of the macabre Algernon Blackwood said that a body changed its cells once every seven years, so he was not the same person he was when conceiving and writing his earlier stories. I'm inclined to agree with both writers: tinkering with early works spoils the raw energy of youth, that naivety that was so refreshing first time around.

When I refer back to the first edition of *The Carpet People*, I feel the original mindset of the author, the awakening of a flat world of possibility – not exactly a discworld but an embryo that needs to grow and absorb more life experience before maturing into the type of novel it was capable of being. Sometimes it's wrong to go back, but pragmatic fans of Pratchett, those who were introduced to *The Carpet People* through the reissue, would argue that I'm wrong. They may be right – it's all subjective. Perhaps nostalgia is a very dangerous thing, but Pratchett always seems to regret that he got his break as a novelist so young, with his first attempt at a novel. One can argue the for and against here, but what is interesting is the opportunity we have had to see the Discworld appear out of the primeval mud of his earlier work. To coin a Lou Reed album title, Pratchett had been 'growing up in public' through his first three novels. They all added to the group of ideas that became *The Colour of Magic*. They defined the fantasy world he was looking for. Interestingly, it was the fantasy world millions of fans around the world were looking for too, but he needed to expel the science fiction genre from his blood first.

The Carpet People is still an ingenious novel from our present viewpoint, showcasing Pratchett's early obsession with genre fiction. He wanted to create a new Narnia, a Middle Earth, all his own. And when the oceans fell tens of thousands of feet off the discworld in *Strata*, his journey to that world was over. But one needs to read the original version of *The Carpet People* to understand that, followed by his two science fiction novels. One could go further and say that one should also read the *Bucks Free Press* stories too, and I will not disagree, because in their own way they explain where the Bromeliad novels came from, for much younger children.

Pratchett's evolution as a novelist has been a methodical one, and the rewriting of *The Carpet People* has obscured that genesis somewhat.

'How careful was I, when I took my way
Each trifle under truest bars to thrust,
That to my use it might unused stay
From hands of falsehood, in sure wards of trust!'
William Shakespeare (*Sonnet 48*)

CHAPTER SEVEN

A Vastly Populated World

'Eight spells go to make up the world. Rincewind knew
that well enough. He knew that the book which
contained them was the Octavo, because it still existed
in the library of the Unseen University – currently
inside a welded iron box at the bottom of a specially
dug shaft, where its magical radiations could be kept
under control.'

(*Eric*)

Followers of the Discworld series find recurring themes, such as
the importance of the number eight, the occupation of a
character's mind by a malignant force – sometimes themselves!
– and the return of many characters and acquaintances within
specific story arcs.*

There are eight days in a disc week and eight colours in its light spectrum. Suffice
to say, eight is a number of magical significance on the Discworld.

There are many characters who populate the Discworld – above and below it, human and otherwise – but some characters have more to do with the history of the Discworld than others. Probably the best example of this is Rincewind. He has travelled the length and breadth of the Discworld, he has fallen off it, and, most importantly, he has travelled back in time to its beginning and visited the creator himself – well, one of them anyway. Sometimes the smaller stories (those that don't bounce around too much or bring in much of the Discworld countryside and history) seem divorced from the series, because they lack the rich and fertile opportunities that the Discworld has created, making the story appear insular and unimportant in comparison.★ This isn't a new observation; the same was said about the TV show *The X-Files*. Any story that had little to do with building the alien conspiracy theory was deemed a lesser story by some fans who were keen to wallow in the bigger picture. This was quite unfair because some of the one-off episodes (such as 'Tooms') were among the most imaginative stories; they broke the mould and got people thinking about the series in a different way, and the same could be said for *The Truth*, *Soul Music* and even *Going Postal* in the Discworld series. In fact, the truth about *The Truth* is it's about journalism and one can quite easily see Pratchett drawing from his 15 years of experience as a journalist to fuel the story. If one ignores the dwarves and vampires, one can see an understanding of the history of journalism in the novel and probably the history of the inside of a pint glass too, as that seems to be a happy pastime for many a roving reporter!

There comes a time when there is only so much that can be said about a specific fantasy world, because too much explanation becomes tedious and takes away some of the

---

I am not including one-off novels in this discussion, or mini-series set outside the Discworld, such as the Johnny Maxwell novels.

mystery. Also, if there is so much speculation over the course of years, the public is never satisfied with whatever pay-off the writer eventually comes up with.*

Returning to *The X-Files*, it got to the stage where the final pay-off wasn't enough, the series having been complicated beyond explanation. But the key to the Discworld is the characters and what they bring to the greater story. For example, it has been speculated by some Pratchett fans that the longest-serving ArchChancellor of the Unseen University, Mustrum Ridcully the Brown, is actually Pratchett himself. With his characteristic hat, staff and white beard, one can detect a strong resemblance, and who else could Pratchett be in the series than the master of the most learned place of Ankh-Morpork? It's so fitting when one appreciates his background and love of writing. Also, by calling him 'the Brown', Pratchett is parodying Gandalf the Grey from *The Lord of the Rings*, but even Gandalf looks like Ridcully and quite possibly Pratchett too! (What about Lord Vetinari with his black clothing and death's-head walking stick? Surely Pratchett in his Discworld manifestation.)

The characters of the Discworld allow Pratchett to explore different themes. The Night Watch allows Pratchett to tackle crime themes plus deeper subjects such as sectarianism, diversity and race relations and a more methodical type of storyline. The Nac Mac Feegle bring in Gaelic legend and Scottish history – and just a hint of stereotypical Scottish fun. Granny Weatherwax allows druid potions and ancient – and modern – medicines to be discussed. Even the Unseen University librarian allows Pratchett to discuss orangutans (although more about them later).

Quite rightly, Pratchett has stated that he doesn't intend to explain away or conclude the Discworld series.

Pratchett doesn't just keep his influences in the British Isles. With the inclusion of ancient warriors and vampires, there is more than a passing reference to European history. Asian and African history have their place too, Egypt having a major impact on the series. All this keeps the series fresh for Pratchett's legions of fans around the world; everybody can find a bit of their own culture in a Pratchett novel. His vastly populated world has now given him the excuse to tackle most themes and legends.

Although some of the one-off stories do not seem to contribute to the great canvas of Discworld, they still pass relevant comment on our own society, giving a validity that is hard to criticise in the greater scheme of things. If one feels betrayed that one hasn't seen a dragon in a Pratchett fantasy, one has to note that it is not necessary to see it. Pratchett's books don't always follow the traditional path of fantasy. But that's where we miss the point slightly and that's the whole point of this chapter: it is the characters who hold the key to what Pratchett wants to say. They are the 'people' who work out what each story is about, and they are the guides for the reader, which is why it is not important to read the books in sequence. However, if one does so, it will increase one's enjoyment of the rich tapestry and hundreds of characters that make up the Discworld. (The same could also be said for the James Bond novels Pratchett read in his youth.) This correlates with the importance Pratchett gives to teenagers and their choices in his novels. Pratchett is genuinely interested in people, and he is inquisitive and broadminded enough to embrace many walks of life. That's what we see in Ankh-Morpork: multi-cultures. There is no prejudice in Pratchett's writing.

I find the earlier novels in the Discworld series more revealing and consequently more enjoyable, especially when discussing the author. I love the way in which Esk de-sexes wizardry. I love the way Cohen the Barbarian and his entourage destroy the clichés of Robert E Howard (well, overused clichés since those stories were published). Let's stop there for a moment, because it is interesting that great characters in literature continue long after their author's death. It is almost as if nobody else has an original idea. Indeed, Conan the Barbarian had many other adventures after Howard's premature death, and even TV's original series of *Star Trek* finds immortality in novels that keep perpetuating its youth and legend.

> 'Behind an ivory, gold-inlaid writing-table sat a man whose broad shoulders and sun-browned skin seemed out of place among those luxuriant surroundings. He seemed more a part of the sun and winds and high places of the outlands. His slightest movement spoke of steel-spring muscles knit to a keen brain with the co-ordination of a born fighting-man.'
>
> Robert E Howard (*The Phoenix on the Sword*)

In fairness, the imagery of Howard's world was so strong and sexually charged, it influenced artwork and films, let alone its chosen genre, for ever after.

> 'The woman on the horse reined in her weary steed. It stood with its legs wide-braced, its head drooping... The woman drew a booted foot out of the silver stirrup and swung down from the gilt-worked saddle. She made the reins fast to the fork of a sapling, and turned about, hands on her hips, to survey her surroundings.'
>
> Robert E Howard (*Red Nails*)

Suddenly we witness Druellae or Liessa from *The Colour of Magic* (see *The Discworld Graphic Novels,* Doubleday, 2008), overtly sexual but tired of the clichés of their gender all the same. Druellae and Liessa may be small characters but they are at the hub of what Pratchett wanted to say with the whole book. It is iconoclastic and similar to what Spike Milligan would do later when rewriting the Bible:

'And God said, Let there be light; and there was light, but Eastern Electricity Board said He would have to wait until Thursday to be connected.
... And God saw the light and it was good; He saw the quarterly bill and that was not good.'
  Spike Milligan (*The Bible: The Old Testament According to Spike Milligan*)

The speculation of gods and the people who make the Discworld are of great importance to its mythology. They should grow in the reader's mind in order to forge a fuller understanding. When Rincewind takes Eric back to the beginning of time – where the Disc is created and sent into space – aiming at something? – there is one of the creators who, like Slartibartfast in *The Hitchhiker's Guide to the Galaxy*, is just one of the award-winning specialists who made the world. One cannot but suspect that there is a nod towards Douglas Adams there. There is nothing wrong with this – Pratchett has been parodying and thanking writers throughout his career as a novelist – but it is interesting that both Pratchett and Adams shared the same sideways look at life. Many people make a comparison between the writers and they are right to do so. Is there a synergy there, a deeper understanding? No, maybe not – maybe it's an admission that whatever craziness they come up with in regard to life, the universe and everything, it won't be as fantastic or way-out and whimsical as the truth, and what is the truth?

Quite!

'"Hello, Slartibartfast," said Arthur at last.
"Hello, Earthman," said Slartibartfast.
"After all," said Ford, "we can only die once."'
Douglas Adams (*Life, the Universe and Everything*)

CHAPTER EIGHT

Grooving with a Pict

'... Being Found Drunk, Being Found Very Drunk,
Using Offensive Language (taking into account ninety-
seven counts of Using Language That Was Probably
Offensive If Anyone Else Could Understand It),
Committing a Breach of the Peace, Malicious
Lingering...'
(Some of the charges against the Nac Mac Feegle in
The Wee Free Men)

We first meet the Nac Mac Feegle in *The Wee Free Men* (Doubleday, 2003). They are small blue Pictsies (not Pixies) with bright red hair, who wear kilts and like drinking and fighting. In fact they were thrown out of Fairyland for being drunk and disorderly, but endear themselves to a young girl called Tiffany Aching, who is a witch in the making.

Armed with a frying pan and the Nac Mac Feegle, Tiffany enters Fairyland to reclaim her cry-baby younger brother from the Queen of the Fairies. This is a time-honoured fantasy: the elder sister – still juvenile herself – has to fight the frustrations of enduring a younger brother and battle the forces of evil to save him because he *is* her brother. This is *Labyrinth*. It has elements of *The Lion, the Witch and the Wardrobe*. It even has shades of *Alice's Adventures in Wonderland* in its offhand vignettes mustered by dromes (sentinels that propel you into a dream, and dreams within dreams) that trap you and subject you to surreal possibilities. The frustrations of Tiffany Aching are not dissimilar to those of Alice in her wonderland. Another connection is her age and inexperience, but that inexperience is also her strength and saviour as she battles a mature foe with the sharpness and temerity of youth.

This same juvenile inexperience tinged with passion to do the right thing is echoed in Neil Gaiman's *Coraline*, where the unprepared girl is pitted against sadistic parent alter egos. It's present again in *The Wonderful Wizard of Oz* (the novel by Frank L Baum), where the young girl battles her way home from a fantastical dream world – quite extreme in my opinion.

Another strong theme tackled in *The Wee Free Men* is used by Clive Barker in *The Thief of Always*, where a month in the parallel world is a lifetime in the real world (Pratchett first uses this in a more subtle way in *Eric*). Pratchett embraces all of this because ultimately he is challenging the heart of Neverland. Peter Pan wants us all to stay with him, again, in a world where the adults are the bad guys and the youngsters are the good. Is this theme endemic to the fantasy genre? No, it was played out skilfully by Charles Dickens throughout his career, perhaps most expertly in *Oliver Twist*. The children are the good, the adults are the evil, but the good can be corrupted by the evil. But there are guardian angels who provide shades of grey – Mr Brownlow in *Oliver Twist*, Nancy still a child in the same novel – and who can save the children and steer them onto the right path. Dickens taught us that it is important to have the light as well as the darkness, but the Brothers Grimm didn't see it that way (nor did Frank L Baum).

The fantasy genre was born in folklore, and nowhere more obviously than in the basic story threads Pratchett tackles in *The Wee Free Men*, but like all his stories, he brings an element – a very amusing element – to the story that is nothing but undiluted original lunacy: the Nac Mac Feegle themselves. As usual he plays with names, making the poet McGonagall immortal in the equally terrible mouse-pipes player William the Gonnagle (a gonnagle is the clan's bard and battle poet). Then there is Rob Anybody, Big Yan, Daft Wullie and Not-as-big-as-Medium-Sized-Jock-but-bigger-than-Wee-Jock-Jock.* These are tragic characters if we believe the boy Roland (who is trapped in Fairyland). He explains that if the Queen is very cross with you, she will stare at you and turn you into something terrible, but he could only draw you how terrible by having a lot of 'red and purple crayons'. The very colours of the Nac Mac Feegle? Well, nearly: they are essentially red and blue.

Because of its close proximity to a traditional fairy story, *The Wee Free Men* is sometimes referred to as a children's tale within the Discworld series. Indeed, it is light and humorous and deals with some traditional themes, and the Nac Mac Feegle are delightfully violent in an endearing way. But I would challenge a later book in the series, *I Shall Wear Midnight*, which tackles more adult themes, as not really being a children's novel (adopting the label 'young adult' instead). In that sense *The Wee Free Men* trilogy betrays its younger readers by its series growing up too quickly. The three books do not form a comfortable

---

Gonnagles don't spend all their time in the same clan. They move around among clans, making sure the songs and stories get spread around to other Nac Mac Feegle.

Johnny and the Bomb-type trilogy. Pratchett doesn't set his sights so narrowly, which raises the question: did the publisher insist upon a Discworld book for young adults to begin with? It matters little now, but the important thing to remember is that, unlike the *Johnny and the Bomb* trilogy, *The Wee Free Men* trilogy is part of a bigger series – Discworld – and the momentum of that series brings other sub-themes and legends into play, diluting the humour and creating further opportunities for expansion along the way.

Going back to the Queen of Fairyland, her porcelain features – so perfect and white – take on an ice-queen quality from *The Chronicles of Narnia*, but then Pratchett informs us of her bright red lips and suddenly vampire-like themes are suggested. The Queen – not unlike the terrible sweet-sucking child she has kidnapped – is spoilt and selfish, and again there are shades of Narnia with Edmund, his Turkish delight and his anger at his siblings. And just like the children in Narnia, Tiffany Aching grows up quickly to thwart her foe.

Many of Pratchett's main characters are endearing because of their innocence. Tiffany, in a similar way to Rincewind, is not convinced of her magical powers, but she grows to understand that they are there within her. Rincewind had to conjure the magic within himself in *The Light Fantastic* and Tiffany is forced to do a similar thing – eventually – spurred on by her little blue friends who crave chaos. In one memorable scene they stay in a very dangerous dream to drink the place dry, having gone to the lengths of taking off the tartan and wearing dinner suits to get at the food and drink. 'I've been facing the Queen and you've been in a *pub*?' Tiffany exclaims in one outburst.

But she has grown, she has taken responsibility, she has come to terms with her own powers and become more of the person she is capable of being, away from the comfort of childhood. And that's the important part of the story: the magic within her is her inner self waking up, not real hocus-pocus magic but a more adult perception. More of her adult mind is showcased when her young brother says 'Big fishy!' when seeing a whale for the first time. Tiffany corrects him like an adult, telling him that it is a common mistake but the whale is actually a mammal.

The updating of the child-snatching Queen of the Fairies/King of the Goblins scenario was another great success for Pratchett, but when Tiffany began to understand how she must earn her pointy witch's hat, it became obvious that Pratchett would follow up his tale of Tiffany and the Nac Mac Feegle. *A Hat Full of Sky* (2004) arrived the very next year; just like Rincewind, Tiffany Aching had an instant sequel. This continuation of a series – or sub-series – within Discworld shows Pratchett's enthusiasm for continuing with a winning set of characters. There's something obsessive about his behaviour in the way he wants to follow a train of thought through to its natural conclusion – if it has one – which may explain why the Nac Mac Feegle have turned up quite often since.* Four times in seven years is a good average. But they're great fun, as *A Hat Full of Sky* continues to show, poking fun at time-honoured scenarios and classic imagery (such as witches having remedies for farmhouses falling on them – very *Wizard of Oz*).

A Hat Full of Sky is a more reserved book than *The Wee Free Men*. It's more thought-provoking and looks in more depth into the characters and the hidden worlds and secrets of the Nac Mac Feegle. Throughout the first hundred pages, the Nac Mac Feegle do nothing outrageous. Rob Anybody marries a Kelda of his own race – not Tiffany Aching – although the Kelda demands that Tiffany is protected against a dangerous Hiver (entity) that is stalking her.

Witness *Strata* followed by The *Colour of Magic*. The good idea of the Discworld was quickly built upon.

It is clear through the first book that Tiffany needed to learn more about her latent powers and the art of becoming a witch, so *A Hat Full of Sky* is an exploration of this learning process. Because the book is slower and less humorous than its predecessor, I would suggest that it is less likely to keep children riveted to the page. What works best about the Nac Mac Feegle is their ability to cause chaos and still find time to misbehave even further while doing so. They are not unlike the household pet that does something stupid or mildly rude in polite company.

A Hat Full of Sky doesn't have the same remit as *The Wee Free Men*. It is a book about relationships, even those within the Nac Mac Feegle. When Jenny tells husband Rob Anybody that she doesn't want him to fight because of their future children, he gives her his word that he won't. But then, as the Kelda of the tribe, she orders him to go into battle (she needs to know that he is loyal to her above anything else, and he shows that mettle). Jenny instantly disliked Tiffany Aching because Rob had been briefly 'engaged' to her, but when Jenny understands that he will put her first, she calms down. There is none of this character-building in the first book. Like *The Colour of Magic*, *The Wee Free Men* was a romp through the imagination and humour conjured by the Discworld, while both sequels (*The Light Fantastic* and *A Hat Full of Sky*) dig deeper into the depths of Pratchett's imagination and allow him to look more objectively at magic and its forgotten secrets. The pages of an ancient book about Hivers are a thought-provoking glimpse into this area of *A Hat Full of Sky*. The books explains that if you allow a Hiver into your mind it will eat it away and break it down.

Is a Hiver a tangible form of brain disease? Is dementia the imagination unleashed, the inability to keep one's own powers at bay? An interesting concept in hindsight, and something we see in creative people from the Victorian artist Richard Dadd (mentioned at the end of *The Wee Free Men*) to Vincent van Gogh; even Wilkie Collins if you want to go back in time in the field of literature.

Pratchett's ability to mix real-world legends in with his fiction is one of his most endearing traits. He won't uncover the secrets of magic in his novels, but he can provide ingenious and challenging ideas that tease and tantalise the reader with their possibilities. This ability to make convincing arguments is a major part of his magic and something that has always been present in his work, even in the early days.

Returning to *A Hat Full of Sky*, there are some interesting things that happen to Tiffany – her life lessons, experiences and learning about her witchcraft – but this pushes the Nac Mac Feegle into the background a little more when they should be the stars of the show. 'Crivens!' they cry, assuring everyone that they really aren't swearing, but one does get suspicious when they're told that they got thrown out of Fairyland for being 'pished' at two in the afternoon – pished meaning 'tired'. It is lines like this that earn the endorsement 'for children of all ages'!

Perhaps the great shame about *A Hat Full of Sky* is the obvious comparison with the Harry Potter series. If we are talking about a witch learning to be a witch and going shopping with like-minded friends to special witch shops, one cannot fail to draw a connection with Harry Potter. One could explore this comparison a little more and say that the Unseen University was around before the Harry Potter stories, but then Jill Murphy's *The Worst Witch* could claim a similar thing. What matters most isn't who or what came first, it's the need to have schools for witches and wizards in modern fantasy novels. Like the vampire novels in the horror genre, the fantastic stories of witches and wizards are dictated by cultural trends. *Dracula* was really the amalgamation of lots of gothic imagery that came before it, and the vampire progressed from this stake in the ground (sorry, couldn't resist it) with novels such as *Interview with the Vampire*, *Buffy the Vampire Slayer* and *Twilight* (and one can add many a Hammer Horror film into that influence too).

Perhaps one could start the progress of schools of witchcraft from early metaphorical 'learning' by child heroes in books such as E Nesbit's *The Phoenix and the Carpet*, through to *The Chronicles of Narnia*. As we can see from these books, and others such as *Twilight, Harry Potter, The Worst Witch*, the Tiffany Aching novels, *The Lord of the Rings* (Frodo and Sam at least), *His Dark Materials, The Scarecrow and his Servant,* even *Aladdin* – I could go on but this is enough for your sanity – children are learning all the time. They are learning the difference between right and wrong, good and evil, fantasy and reality. Essentially, through their adventures they are learning to grow up, to arm themselves with the tools that will make them wise adults. The children who read these books and pick up on the moral undertones will learn alongside their favourite characters. And there lies a very interesting distinction between science fiction and fantasy: science fiction is about the advancement of a race; fantasy can be about the advancement of a child's imagination, to learn perception and to think outside the box. Think about the great artists throughout history, they have all used imagination – a fundamental part of the fantasy genre – to push back the boundaries and stand out; people as diverse as David Bowie, Spike Milligan, Charles Dickens and Vincent van Gogh. That's an eclectic bunch, but they all supposedly went too far with their technicolour imaginations. That's where true innovation lies, and innovation is at the hub of the fantasy genre, and when somebody comes up with something original a classic is made.

'"The message is this. Don't go through the door."
He paused.

"Does that mean anything to you?"
"No," said Coraline.
The old man shrugged.'

                                   Neil Gaiman (*Coraline*)

There are great fantasy creators around today, and it is not surprising that they work in a variety of media to makes their vivid dreams come true. Neil Gaiman and Clive Barker have used comic books, novels, art and films to express their ideas and landscapes. Pratchett has learned to do much the same, allowing his stories to be adapted for theatre too. Clive Barker started out in the theatre with his horror stories, and that is where he learned much about his audience and how to work them. Pratchett's first audience was children: his peers at school and then the younger readers of the *Bucks Free Press*. When one looks at the wide body of work Pratchett has produced, one can see clear children's series, such as the Bromeliad trilogy (*Truckers, Diggers* and *Wings*) and the Tiffany Aching series (*The Wee Free Men, A Hat Full of Sky, Wintersmith* and *I Shall Wear Midnight*), which got too dark to be purely for children. And that is an important area we need to explore within Pratchett's work.

CHAPTER NINE

Challenging the Cliché

'They may be called the Palace Guard, the City Guard...
Whatever the name, their purpose in any work of
heroic fantasy is identical: it is, round Chapter Three...
to rush into the room, attack the hero one at a time,
and be slaughtered. No one ever asked them if they
wanted to.'

(Dedication, *Guards! Guards!*)

We've witnessed it in every swashbuckling movie ever made,
from Errol Flynn's *Robin Hood* through Burt Lancaster's *The
Crimson Pirate* and *The Flame and the Arrow* to Johnny Depp's
Pirates of the Caribbean: the hordes of unnamed guards who get
killed senselessly. As Pratchett says above, nobody asked them if
they wanted to be a guard, but nevertheless as lower, more
worthless beings, they are killed off for the thrill of the
swashbuckler in the name of adventure. Only once in movies
have we seen the loss and trauma caused by these wanton acts:

in *Austin Powers: International Man of Mystery*. After a wave of violence at Doctor Evil's establishment, soldiers are killed off in various ways. We then cut to their homes and witness the effect their death has on their families. OK, so it's a comedy film, but then most swashbuckling movies are light family entertainment, and it's the not-taking-this-seriously aspect that pulls the action away from poignant real life, and that's exactly where Pratchett is with the action-packed *Guards! Guards!*

> 'Once you've ruled out the impossible then whatever is left, however improbable, must be the truth... There was also the curious incident of the orangutan in the night-time...'
>
> (*Guards! Guards!*)

In *Guards! Guards!* there is a moment of detection when Captain Vimes has to work out where the dragon is nesting, and at exactly this point we witness Pratchett parodying the greatest detective of them all – Sherlock Holmes (see the quote above). There is no sacred turf for the classics where Pratchett is concerned.

In the Discworld's Ankh-Morpork there is immense danger on the streets, especially late at night. As a result there are laws – for the Night Watch – such as Not Arresting Thieves, especially ringleaders, but Carrot, a new dwarf recruit (well, a dwarf over six feet tall), is not aware of such unspoken rules and ends up on the receiving end of a very big learning curve that upsets the equilibrium of the city. Very soon there is more trouble than can possibly be imagined, as Carrot tries to do his job by the book and not let his Night Watch mentor show him the ropes. But dwarves – even those over six feet tall – are an ethnic minority and therefore have rights.

Through Captain Sam Vimes and his motley crew, Pratchett

pokes fun at the craziness of the law as well as the injustice of the slaughtered trillions in books and movies past. Again, this is the iconoclastic Pratchett at his best, and it is no wonder that *Guards! Guards!* is the book he most wants to see produced into a movie, which would make a refreshing change, as the guards wouldn't get mercilessly slaughtered for a change.

> '**Ankh-Morpork didn't rear. Rather it sort of skulked, clinging to the soil as if afraid someone might steal it. There were no flags.**'
>
> (*Guards! Guards!*)

The quote above could be from an Ian Rankin novel, where he describes the Jekyll and Hyde imagery of the city of Edinburgh at night. But no, the author is Terry Pratchett and the city is Ankh-Morpork, with the unpredictability of any great city and the obligatory dangers that lie within. To combat those dangers, Pratchett has to populate it with police officers, especially after dark – the Night Watch – who want to save their own skin and not combat crime in any way. It will never be thwarted, so why bother? Perhaps Ian Rankin's Inspector Rebus should have thought the same way. He was never going to conquer crime, so why did he put his head on the block so many times? Why did he hit the bottle? Indeed, why did Sam Vimes do a similar thing, especially if he didn't care? There is much to appreciate in Pratchett's crime-busting (sic) novels, because not only do they show crime as endemic, they show the preposterous red tape that officials are up against if they want to make one positive change – so what's the bloody use?

> '"This is Lord Mountjoy Quickfang Winterforth IV, the hottest dragon in the city. It could burn your head clean off... Now I know what you're thinking," Vimes went

on, softly. "You're wondering, after all this excitement, has it got enough flame left? And, y'know, I ain't sure myself.'"

(Guards! Guards!)

I've used the word before, but iconoclast describes a person who challenges the widely accepted and brings down accepted institutions. Here is our open door to speak about the Terry Pratchett who has Alzheimer's disease, and the steps he is taking to stop the disease, or at least make people aware of it and start to combat it.

Pratchett wasn't going to quietly accept the fact that he had the disease. He wanted to use his position as a respected author to make people take notice of it and understand it as something that is not uncommon but is sadly overlooked (compared with a disease such as cancer). But from there he took things on to another level, talking about assisted death. Is this Pratchett's obsessiveness coming through again? Possibly, but in fairness it is something that is very close to home on this occasion.

'Edinburgh slept on, as it had slept for hundreds of years. There were ghosts in the cobbled alleys and on the twisting stairways of the Old Town tenements, but they were enlightened ghosts, articulate and deferential.'

Ian Rankin (Knots and Crosses)

Something *Guards! Guards!* has, which no Ian Rankin book features, is dragons. Pratchett explains their absence from the real world by stating that they have been lying dormant, waiting to be awoken by a special key.

Although dragons are stock-in-trade for the fantasy genre, Pratchett doesn't just accept their presence because he is writing fantasy. He explains their absence and, by doing so, implies that they may well have lived and breathed – fire – sometime in our own world's history. This is a trick missed by Tolkien, as the great dragon Smaug was an accepted fact for the Hobbit and his friends. Pratchett is always questioning the world around him, sometimes subtly but at other times with more anger.

> '"No bloody flying newt sets fire to my city,"
> said Vimes.'

> (*Guards! Guards!*)

CHAPTER TEN

The Dreams and Nightmares of Childhood

'He was a genius, of course. It's a word that gets tossed around a lot these days, and it's used to mean pretty much anything. But Douglas was a genius, because he saw the world differently, and more importantly, he could communicate the world he saw. Also, once you'd seen it his way you could never go back.'

Neil Gaiman ('Foreword: What Was He Like, Douglas Adams?', *The Ultimate Hitchhiker's Guide to the Galaxy*)

In Dickens' day, to say that somebody had a genius for something was implying that they were extremely good at it – whatever it was. Neil Gaiman has called Douglas Adams a genius and I'm sure without too much prompting he would call Terry Pratchett a genius for much the same reason. But what I find intriguing about Pratchett is that, like Roald Dahl, he can easily reach into childhood. It is as though there is a clear, brightly lit corridor that takes him straight there. Not necessarily *back* there

– just there. On the one occasion I met Dahl he told me that he didn't know where his ability to write children's stories came from. As I was 11 years old at the time, I found that a little puzzling, but I think a similar thing applies to Pratchett. The children's book is just a macabre sub-genre to the main track of his imagination. For Dahl, it was his brilliantly crafted short stories; for Pratchett it is his darkly set Discworld books. The darkness is clearly seen through the character of Death and, to a degree, the Night Watch. The seedy side of life intrigues some writers, witness Charles Dickens, who had a direct link to the pain of his childhood in the same way that John Lennon did. But you wouldn't get Dahl, Pratchett – or even Douglas Adams – screaming for his mother as Lennon did. That mental scar was never there.

In his autobiography *The Fry Chronicles*, Stephen Fry talks about visiting Adams and the frustrations he could hear emanating from the study upstairs as he pained over a paragraph. Perhaps that was an occasion when he could have called out for his mother, but he probably decided to swear and curse instead. The point I'm making here is that Adams, like Milligan when writing *The Goon Show*, agonised over every sentence because what he was doing was different and cutting edge. Pratchett, through the sheer volume of his output and apparent lack of screaming or pain, has had an easier time of it overall, but the comparison with Adams is still there. Does that make him a greater genius – that so over-used word – or does it hark back to Dickensian times and suggest that he is simply very good at what he does?

There is a tendency to package things nowadays, to present a ready-made meal to the consumer and get the money in the door. I have spoken about the differences in genre, but at the same time there are people pushing the boundaries and creating something else that can still be set within a genre but is as detached from it as it is attached to it. *The Hitchhiker's Guide to the Galaxy* is a prime example – it has as much humour as science fiction – but the Discworld series did as much in the fantasy genre.

The imagination can take many swerves and sometimes that swerve can go down the corridor of youth. In fantasy this is a much easier thing to do, because the imagery of a magical fairytale land is much closer, as dragons, dwarves and witches beckon with gnarled talons.

I will discuss Pratchett's children's novels in a separate chapter, but there is an important aspect to cover first: the influence of childhood in adult books. This has been an important theme in the horror/chiller fiction of James Herbert over the years, especially in the David Ash trilogy, but even though Pratchett doesn't over-egg the childhood influence omelette too much, there is a very important section at the beginning of a Discworld book that needs some discussion here. It's a place where the dreams and nightmares of childhood still reverberate: *Hogfather*.

'It's the night before Hogwatch. And it's too quiet.'
(Hogfather)

The 'oh god of hangovers', *someone* coming down the chimney with a sack instead of a scythe, and the immortal words 'ho, ho, ho' – it can only be Hogwatch! But is Hogwatch nothing more than a satire of Christmas?

I would be disappointed if that were so, because Hogwatch was mentioned as an aside *before* the Discworld series. When Pratchett eventually came around to writing a book dedicated to Hogwatch – which to this day reminds me of Dr Seuss's Grinch – a cornucopia of ideas poured out of the opening few pages, opening Pratchett's previously locked door of children's dreams and nightmares. And he starts right at the very beginning, when the Discworld was young and the things that create tradition and history come from something as free form as… well, free form: 'Things just happen. What the hell.'

History moves forwards and tradition takes on a tangible existence through the repetition of life. So there really is a monster in the cellar and the governess has to grab it and throw it out in order for the child to go back to bed, and that's exactly what happens. It was all in a day's work – well, night's – because the monster would evaporate by dawn.

The magic of Christmas, the mysteries of night, the thin line between a child's dreams and nightmares – and then the plain reality of life that echoes the best and worst hopes and fears of childhood: Hogwatch. The good, the bad, the ugly of life: *Hogfather*.

Hogfather was a book that needed to be written. It was the macabre place Pratchett had to go in order to illustrate the realities of growing up, and how the irrational fears of childhood are translated into the harsh realities of adulthood.

'And then there was only the snow.
After a while, it began to melt in the sun.'

(Hogfather)

Since the dawn of time, every human being has been born of woman, lived and died. Some have had children along the way and made some contribution to the legacy of the human race. But why is it, without prompt, that a child will run from the bathroom once they have turned the light out at night, just as their parents did, just as their grandparents had done, without any true reason to do so, without any real justification?

For me, this is where Pratchett wins the biggest points because he supposes that somewhere way back in time, somebody had the wildest and biggest scare possible and the legacy of that has been passed down genetically through countless generations.

> '... and there presently rose to my nostrils the subtle, penetrating perfume of age: of letters, long preserved, with ink faded and ribbon pale; of scented tresses, golden and brown, laid away, ah, how tenderly! among pressed flowers that still held the inmost delicacy of their forgotten fragrance; the scented presence of lost memories...'
>
> Algernon Blackwood ('The House of the Past', *Tales of the Uncanny and Supernatural*)

The fear of the unknown, the darkness lost in the mists of time, these are the chilling – thrilling – factors that create suspense, wonder and intrigue. These are the ingredients that make bestselling novels and hit movies. And to be thrilled is better than the need to be horrified: that is the difference between the need for make-believe and the horrors of reality, present-day or ancient.

> 'They were sounds that I had heard many times before in my life, and yet they were still, for me, the most thrilling and evocative in the whole world. They consisted of a series of little soft metallic noises, of metal grating gently against metal, and they were made, they were always made by somebody who was very slowly, very cautiously, turning the handle of one's door from the outside.'
>
> Roald Dahl ('The Visitor', *Switch Bitch*)

CHAPTER ELEVEN

If Music be the Food of Love

'Other children got given xylophones. Susan just had to ask her grandfather to take his vest off.'

(Soul Music)

The dark majesty of the music of Thomas Tallis in a piece such as 'Spem in Alium' ('Life in Any Other' – a piece for eight choirs of five voices) exposes the gentleness and calm at the centre of Pratchett's life. The author rates the 16th-century English composer highly and, if one looks at the almost Amish-like whites and blacks of Pratchett's taste in clothing and interior design, one can detect a love of more conservative and simple times.

Tallis was an Elizabethan composer who wrote music to please his queen and the nation as a whole. His pieces are now considered to be best suited for grand cathedrals and state occasions. He was not a composer in the style of Bach or Mozart; he lived and wrote in a time when the music of heavenly choirs was more sought after than that of instruments. Simple beauty is something that appeals to Pratchett, and for a spiritual person – rather than a deeply religious one – he shows his empathy for assumed religious music through compositions adopted by it.

Simplicity in music has created highly praised milestones in different genres throughout history, witness 'Silent Night' or John Lennon's 'Imagine'. Things don't have to be complicated. Ask any writer – draft number one is normally better than draft number 56, because the meaning isn't obscured by too many metaphors or similes.

> 'The person on the other side was a young woman. Very obviously a young woman. There was no possible way that she could have been mistaken for a young man in any language, especially Braille.'
>
> *(Maskerade)*

See what I mean! When people talk about the secret of writing a bestseller, the obvious answer is KISS (Keep It Simple Stupid). Write what you know about and don't try too hard are the watchwords. When you open a book, the voice of the author should be there, and all the great writers have that ability to engage with their own voice, from Frederick Forsyth to Julia Donaldson.

> 'The wind howled. The storm crackled on the mountains. Lightning prodded the crags like an old man trying to get an elusive blackberry pip out of his false teeth.'
>
> *(Maskerade)*

The voice of your favourite author is as comfortable and reassuring as a favourite shirt, a reliable old pair of shoes; instantly you get it, and want to be part of the new adventure, and there is an effortlessness that draws you across the pages and from the front of the book to the back. Pratchett found this with authors such as Tolkien, and now many people find it with him.

In 1997 Pratchett appeared on the radio programme *Desert Island Discs*. His choice of music was eclectic but revealing, citing the traditional song 'Thomas the Rhymer' by Steeleye Span as his favourite track. Steeleye Span are an English folk-rock band, initially formed in 1969. Best known for their 1975 hit 'All Around My Hat', they are, along with Fairport Convention, one of the best known bands of the British folk revival and a world away from Thomas Tallis, but then again so were some of Pratchett's other choices, from Vivaldi and Mozart to the Australian band Icehouse and Meat Loaf. And it's with the last-mentioned artist that we see a strong comparison with Pratchett's fiction: the character Death on his motorbike evoking the famous image of Meat Loaf's 'Bat Out of Hell' flying out of the stage; indeed, that was the very track Pratchett selected for *Desert Island Discs*.

> '... someone tentatively picked up a musical instrument that echoed to the rhythm in their soul.'
>
> (*Soul Music*)

When it comes to music, Pratchett wears his heart on his sleeve and we see bits of his personality in his choices. It's almost like music influences his personality and shapes his writing – it's certainly an important part of his life. Another of his Desert Island Discs was Bernard Miles' 'The Race for the Rhinegold Stakes'. Miles was a writer, actor and director well known for his comic monologues, and one can picture Pratchett and his father listening to him while members of the Chiltern Amateur Radio Club. Like most people his age, Pratchett grew up listening to the radio and enjoying the great comedians of the second part of the 20th century. Great acts such as the Goons and shows such as *Round the Horne*, *The Navy Lark* and *Hancock's Half Hour* would appeal to his irreverent sense of humour.

> "*Dad da da dum!* Doesn't that stir anything in you?"
> **Douglas Adams (Ford Prefect to a Vogan guard,**
> *The Hitchhiker's Guide to the Galaxy***)**

In *Soul Music* Pratchett picks up on the same classical composition as Ford Prefect (above), albeit 'Dah dah dah *DAH*'. It seems there are impressive but simple pieces of music that echo throughout time and space, and are used to such fitting ends by iconoclasts such as Pratchett and Douglas Adams.

Soul Music is drenched in musical goodies. With characters like Cliff and Buddy, one naturally thinks of Cliff Richard and Buddy Holly from the 1950s music scene. And then you have titles such as 'BORN TO RUNE' screaming out at you and simultaneously paying tribute to the iconic 1970s album *Born to Run,* by Bruce Springsteen and the E Street Band.

Of course Death has to get involved, and the threat of playing down at the crossroads to save your soul (not unlike Eric Clapton) becomes a very real possibility, although it fails to show. Pratchett really runs through the history of pop/rock music in *Soul Music*, acutely understanding what makes it tick and therefore striking a chord within people.

With each of his books, Pratchett picks a theme and exploits it fully. He turns all the clichés around and provides the audience with a different take on traditional themes.

'"Live fast. Die young."
The music tugged at his soul.'

(*Soul Music*)

Soul Music pokes fun at popular music and the insatiable lust of youth, exploiting all the clichés along the way. 'Never age. Never die. Live for ever in that one last white-hot moment, when the crowd screamed. When every note was a heartbeat.'

But as with his *Desert Island Discs* choices, Pratchett doesn't just look at popular music of the late 20th century. He goes back and looks at more traditional pockets of music, such as opera, which he deals with in *Maskerade* through a parody of Gaston Leroux's *The Phantom of the Opera*. Yes, of course the chandelier that hangs over the audience is just an accident waiting to happen, but it's not just these tongue-in-cheek asides that drive the book, it is the music too. It is the glue that keeps the soul of the opera house together. Good music – like good books and love – never dies.

Maskerade is a Discworld novel in the witches series and begins with Agnes Nitt leaving Lancre to seek fame and fortune at the opera house in Ankh-Morpork. This is where the paths of influential witches cross. Granny Weatherwax finds out that Nanny Ogg has written a popular cookbook but has not been paid by the publisher. The witches leave Ankh-Morpork to collect the money, as well as attempting to entice Agnes Nitt into their coven.

Agnes becomes a member of the opera house chorus and meets Christine, who begins to get more leading roles because the resident murderous ghost demands it of the management. But all is not as it seems, and murder, dodgy finance and intrigue are rife, echoing the greed and power of the money people behind the music industry in the real world today. One could say that the ghost is only using exploitation, like a maniac agent.

It is interesting that *Maskerade* and *Soul Music* were released close together in the Discworld series, but this is typical Pratchett not letting a train of thought go. He needed to look at certain themes in different ways and this is something we see time and time again in his work. Only when he has got something out of his system does he finally let it go and move on to the next theme. So are *Maskerade* and *Soul Music* inextricably linked? I think so. Both are hugely enjoyable novels about music and the influence it has on people and, when we see the favouritism for Christine in *Maskerade*, we assume that favouritism through attraction will always outshine talent, and indeed Agnes is the victim in this situation.

> "'I mean, everyone acts as if it's only the music that matters! The plots don't make sense! Half the stories rely on people not recognising their servants or wives because they've got a tiny mask on! Large ladies play the part of consumptive girls! No one can act properly!... There should be a sign on the door saying 'Leave your common sense here'! If it wasn't for the music the whole thing would be ridiculous!'"

> (*Maskerade*)

Pratchett casts a pessimistic eye over the world of opera in *Maskerade*, which is something he doesn't really do in *Soul Music*. He seems more in tune with pop and rock music than opera, and that is clearly shown through his *Desert Island Discs* selection as well.

Pratchett rounded off his desert island experience by selecting *Edible Plants of the South Seas* by Emile Massal as his book of choice, clearly a practical selection, but still showing his love of horticulture. Picking New York's Chrysler Building as his luxury item was probably taking fantasy a step too far!

CHAPTER TWELVE

The Long Dark Tea Party of the Soul

'"As though Nature... here and there concealed
vacuums, gaps, holes in space (his mind was always
speculative; more than speculative, some said)..."'
Algernon Blackwood ('*Entrance and Exit*')

Lots of writers have a morbid fascination with the darker side of life. We see this most prevalently in crime, horror, science fiction and fantasy writing. It's as though people are only entertained if there is a darkness – an evil – that people have to do battle with. One could suggest that this is society's call for more bloodshed, since the explicitness of the horror genre dates from the early to mid-1970s with the arrival of Stephen King and James Herbert. But why should we blame those guys? Explicit horror has been around since mankind could dream in technicolour.

But it's not gore I want to explore here, it is Darkness with a capital D. The Darkness of Poe, Dickens, Shelley, Stoker, Doyle and Stevenson – some call it gothic or macabre but they're wrong – is the crux of page-turning mystery, and by mystery I mean an audience's desire to know what happens next. It's where I believe Dan Brown has got it all wrong. If *The Da Vinci Code* and *Angels and Demons* had been dark rather than horrific, they would have been much better books. There are of course books that need horror, such as *The Rats* and *Lair* (from James Herbert's *The Rats* trilogy), but even he brought in other elements in *Domain* (the series' finale) to create one of his most exciting and thought-provoking novels.

There are some novels, however, that exploit the Darkness beautifully – with Herbert, witness *Others* – but there is also Stephen Laws' *Macabre* and the lesser-known novel *The Pastor* by Philip Trewinnard. Moving away from horror and into fantasy, we can witness the Darkness in *Coraline* (Neil Gaiman), *The Thief of Always* (Clive Barker) and *I Shall Wear Midnight* by Terry Pratchett. Every book is a field day for movie director Tim Burton because he understands how the Darkness should be played, *Edward Scissorhands* and *The Corpse Bride* being very good examples. The same can be said within the science fiction genre. Looking at *Doctor Who* alone, 'The Empty Child', 'Blink' and '42' are fine examples of how Darkness is conjured within the show's comeback seasons with Christopher Eccleston and David Tennant.

Let us now explore the Darkness in the mindset of Terry Pratchett with regard to the Tiffany Aching novels. *The Wee Free Men* was a children's book, *A Hatful of Sky* and *Wintersmith* less so, but *I Shall Wear Midnight* definitely not. Why is that? Because it harbours the Darkness.

'She got one hour's sleep before the nightmare began.'
(*I Shall Wear Midnight*)

Pratchett lives at a slower pace nowadays. Whether that is because of the diagnosis of his Alzheimer's or just the process of getting older is unclear. He admitted to *The Times* in May 2011 that he pays 'more attention to the details of nature now. I tend to see things more clearly in the garden, which is totally contradictory [to the symptoms of his Alzheimer's]. I'll see the details in the flowers or the birds and things like that.'

This is a very telling quote. There is so much one overlooks in everyday life, which one takes for granted, and this has been an important theme in Pratchett's work over the years. Algernon Blackwood was very much influenced by Earth Power and the unseen doorways in nature (see 'Entrance and Exit', 'The Willows', 'The Wendigo', 'A Haunted Island' and even 'The House of the Past'). As Pratchett walked through his garden during *The Times* interview, one almost expected the Nac Mac Feegle to make an appearance, and indeed the conversation goes exactly that way, with Pratchett saying that the day after his Alzheimer's was diagnosed he thought he saw '"a pixie in a red hat". He looked away and told himself that it must have been a flower or some red leaves. But when he looked at the spot again, there was no flower, no red leaves.'

Tiffany Aching once said that one day she would wear midnight – to be a qualified witch – and perhaps Pratchett is proving himself equally worthy. He did go on to say that he didn't really think it was a pixie and therefore didn't tell anybody about his experience. But there is a very important point here. The Bible tells us about all that is seen and unseen, and added to that should be the things we choose not to see or appreciate in everyday life. It's as though human conditioning takes away the power that allows us to stop and look more deeply into what lies around us, which probably explains why children normally have the natural power of second sight and not adults.

'But somewhere – some time – there's a tangled ball of evil and spite, of hatred and malice, that has woken up. And it's waking up all the old stories too – stories about evil old witches.'

(Jacket blurb, *I Shall Wear Midnight*)

Tiffany Aching is now a witch caring for the sick and elderly, but because she deals with people, she sees the Darkness that festers inside the home. People open up to her and talk about the darker side of life. She tries to hold back – but that's the only place where she will find the power to wear midnight.

'"… If you chopped your hand off I could probably make you forget about it until you tried to eat your dinner, but things like loss, grief and sadness? I can't do that. I wouldn't *dare* meddle with them. There is something called 'the soothing', and I know only one person in the world who can do that, and I'm not even going to ask her to teach me. It's too deep."'

(*I Shall Wear Midnight*)

The thing that really intrigues me about *I Shall Wear Midnight* is the *progression* of magic. Tiffany Aching is proving herself to be a witch of power. She is tackling adult problems, the darker areas of life that exist after youth and are influenced by stress, relationship problems, ill health and downright cruelty. These are issues that haven't appeared in Pratchett's novels before, not in a real everyday sense. Domestic violence thwarted by magic, or a negotiation of things that could be construed as magic if performed by a witch, shows a maturity for Tiffany Aching, a girl who has learned important lessons in life. Early in the book, she talks about learning from her elders, not just Granny Weatherwax but Nanny Ogg too. This is akin to a teenager

Sir Terry Pratchett at home in 2010, proudly holding a sword he forged from scratch. © *Rex Features*

Andrew Falvey, Brian Blessed, George Baker and other member of the cast of the 1995 children's TV series *Johnny and the Dead*, based on Pratchett's novel.

© *Rex Features*

Above: Terry Pratchett at the Cheltenham Literature Festival in 1996.

Below: Signing copies of *Carpe Jugulum* at a party in 1999 celebrating the opening of the flagship branch of Waterstone's in Piccadilly, London.

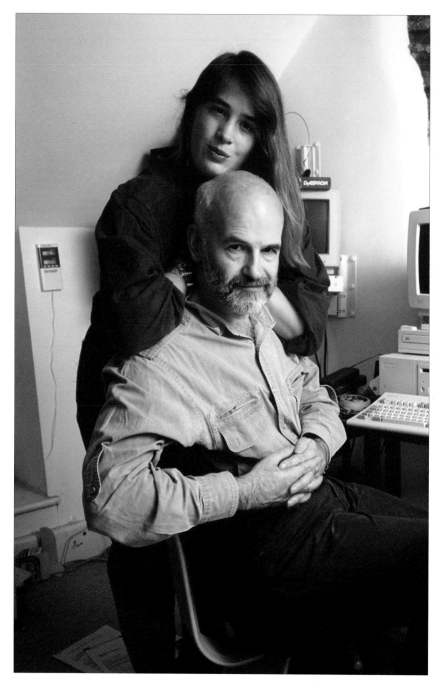

Pratchett at home with his daughter Rhianna in 1998.   © *Rex Features*

At a *Going Postal* signing in Cardiff in May 2005.   © *Rex Features*

Above: Pictured with David Jason in November 2006 at the premiere of the TV adaptation of *Hogfather*.

Below: On set during production of *The Colour of Magic* in 2007.

Above: At home near Salisbury in Wiltshire.

Below: With fans at the Somerset town of Wincanton in 2009 for the unveiling of a series of road names inspired by the Discworld series.

Above left: Sir Terry Pratchett receiving his knighthood in 2009.

Above right: Author Neil Gaiman, who has worked extensively with Pratchett, pictured at the Edinburgh Book Festival in 2011.

Below: Photographed at the 2011 Chelsea Flower Show in London.

listening to the life philosophy of their grandparents. This is confirmed by Tiffany admitting to herself that Nanny Ogg was good at old magic, which was magic that didn't need witches and was built into the landscape and concerned death, marriage, betrothals and the promises never spoken out loud; fundamental things older people knew about.

> 'You didn't need to be a witch to understand it. The world around you became more – well, more fluid, at those special times.'
>
> (*I Shall Wear Midnight*)

If we recognise this deeper magic alongside Pratchett's ability to see more in his garden, to stop and reflect just that one iota more, then we observe that it is his maturity as a writer that has fuelled the deeper perception of Tiffany Aching and the people of the Discworld. He has made them grow up too. Too quickly? Probably not, but the onset of Alzheimer's would make him aware of his own mortality and could press him closer to the culmination of certain story arcs, such as the end of the Tiffany Aching series with *I Shall Wear Midnight*.

There is a clear way forwards at the end of the Tiffany Aching quartet. She is a witch of a large area now. Her time isn't her own. She muses about marriage and notes that many witches didn't get married because they didn't have the time, and the ones who did (with the exception of Nanny Ogg) only dealt with herbs thereafter. One could say that this is a good parallel to many career women in the modern world, but when Pratchett announces that 'Witches were definitely women', one can cast a thought back to Esk and wonder where that conformity came from.

Witches are a breed apart. They are different from other people: they hold secrets, they are needed in times of great

sorrow and great joy, and that leads us back to the priesthood. The people of the Chalk needed a witch and so Tiffany Aching decided to become one. Was it really her calling, or was it something she just fell into? Ask a thousand civil servants in the real world and work out the answer yourself; people don't necessarily adopt the Civil Service as their first-choice career, not unless they are destined for great things. But Tiffany flies high in the sky where no one can see her tears. She wakes from a nightmare and we learn of the Darkness of family life: Mr Petty got drunk, Mrs Petty ran from the house screaming because Mr Petty beat his daughter so hard she lost her baby… and Mr Petty's hands had bunched up because he always thought with his fists not his mind.

So Mr Petty was very bad and very wrong, but his daughter was only 13. Should she have been pregnant in the first place? The response to all this is scary and not for any child to understand: 'Are you trying to tell me that she was too young for a bit of romance, but young enough to be beaten so hard that she bled from places where no one should bleed?'

In his Author's Note, Pratchett admits that the best way to make things up is to make them out of real things. *I Shall Wear Midnight* comes from some of those real things, things that are whispered in corners and not spoken of openly. In the book, Tiffany Aching responds to prejudice, to meddling in things she shouldn't. She deals with bad people and levels of evil and cruelty. All that is at the very heart of the story. It is a book about facing up to the Darkness and doing something about it, and when people do that they question whether they are wrong or right for making the decisions they make. There is never a clear-cut answer, and ultimately Tiffany Aching feels the same way. She ends up a witch of power, but at what cost?

Is there a purpose to all the heartache? In *Eric* – an early novel in the series – when Rincewind witnessed the birth of the

Discworld, it appeared to have a purpose, somewhere for the great turtle to swim towards. I love this idea, because it gives purpose to the creature, something that justifies its single-minded flight through the heavens. There was a purpose with *The Light Fantastic* and there should be further purpose. The greater canvas of the Discworld needs tightening, but does it need a purpose and an overall direction for the people who live there? A meaning to life? As if the world and all its people were created for a wonderful purpose? And there we find our way back to God, which doesn't sit well with the series' creator. It is the randomness of the Discworld that works, the layers of importance and uselessness, because that echoes reality on its grandest canvas. One shouldn't think of Discworld in comparison to the fantasies of other writers; one should look upon it as something more free-form and as unfathomable as everyday life. The closest comparison I can give is Anthony Powell's *A Dance to the Music of Time* series, where characters drop in and out of each other's lives over a course of years to small or large extents, but there is a greater synergy to the series because it echoes the free-form day-to-day lives of everyday people, the observations that are nothing but recorded vignettes of custom and desire.

What am I ultimately saying about the Discworld series? That it shouldn't have been for children. Fantasy should have been the genre and adult themes should have been the backbone to a revealing parallel world of Darkness and the macabre. In a way, Pratchett couldn't shake Uncle Jim from his *Bucks Free Press* days, or maybe even before that and the work he presented to his peers at school. Discworld has struggled to offer books ideal for children. Animated versions have been successful, even comic book adaptations, because they water down the detail somewhat and make them more palatable for youngsters. There have been successful books for children such as *The Amazing*

Maurice and his Educated Rodents and *The Wee Free Men* (especially the illustrated edition), but on the whole the core audience starts at the teenage years, the exact age of some of the main characters in the books, who are also making key decisions in their own lives. That's where the magic of Discworld really begins and the self-teaching starts, a self-teaching that lasts throughout one's lifetime.

> 'Harry kept smiling, and waving, even though it was like a bereavement, watching his son glide away from him...'
>
> JK Rowling (*Harry Potter and the Deathly Hallows*)

There is a Bruce Springsteen line in the song 'Two Hearts' (from the album *The River*) that says that people grow up to dream again. Perhaps another side to fantasy isn't just the instruction of moral duties to children, it is the reminder to adults to remember those teachings and pass them on to the younger generation themselves.

CHAPTER THIRTEEN

Writing for Children

'Fairy tales are more than true: not because they tell us
that dragons exist, but because they tell us that dragons
can be beaten.'

GK Chesterton

If Terry Pratchett had never created the Discworld series, he
would still be a celebrated children's writer. When adults
contemplate Pratchett novels for children, they often say
'Aren't they really for older readers?', referring to the
Discworld series. As we've discovered, many of the Discworld
novels are not for young children, but there are some obviously
fine children's books that don't get confused by the Discworld,
such as the Bromeliad trilogy, the Johnny Maxwell trilogy and
Where's My Cow?

Where's My Cow? was a children's picture book released
alongside the Discworld title *Thud!* In *Thud!* the character of
Sam Vimes reads his child a bedtime story about a lost cow and

how she is found by her owner. (As this story is mentioned in *Thud!,* it provides a new story within a story before *The Tales of Beedle the Bard* from *Harry Potter and the Deathly Hallows*.) It is a short, beautifully illustrated book and a complete departure from anything Pratchett had done before. It also showcases his passion for fine illustrations, with several illustrators contributing to the work.

The Bromeliad trilogy is made up of *Truckers* (1990), *Diggers* (1991) and *Wings* (1991). The stories tell of a race of Nomes, who find out that they originally came from another planet and decide that they want to return to it.

The Bromeliad trilogy title is built partly from Homer's *The Iliad* and partly from Bromeliaceae tropical herbs (history and a love of gardening coming into play again). As with the first Discworld titles (or flat world novels if we include *Strata*), we witness a set of books written closely together and dealing with the ongoing adventures of a certain group of characters, in this case Nomes. This concentrated effort of writing a short series of books back to back was repeated with the Johnny Maxwell trilogy. There is a connection between the Bromeliad trilogy and the Johnny Maxwell trilogy, as *Truckers* was set in Johnny's home town of Blackbury (a town first invented in the *Bucks Free Press*), so again we can see interlocking themes, characters and locations spread across different series of books and short stories, which allow different themes to be explored with some familiarity.

The Johnny Maxwell trilogy is one of the most celebrated in Pratchett's canon. The books instantly appeal to children, especially boys around their teenage years, because the characters are essentially of a similar age. Pratchett has said that the books are very loosely based upon Richmal Crompton's *Just William* books, in a 1990s, updated type of way. I don't necessarily agree with this as Johnny is a highly moral young man with special powers of perception, but his mixed bag of friends do evoke the rough-diamond aspects of the William stories: Bigmac (named for obvious reasons), Yo-less (because he never says 'Yo' and is uncool for a black kid) and Wobbler (because of his weight he wobbles when walking) are the main reprobates.

We first meet the characters in *Only You Can Save Mankind*, a highly moralistic tale from the birth of the computer game era.* In the story, Wobbler is a computer game enthusiast who plays a game once, works it out, occasionally changes its rules and manoeuvres, and then passes it on to friends to completely baffle them. Johnny Maxwell believes he's been given a Wobbler special when the aliens in a game called *Only You Can Save Mankind* suddenly surrender and beg him to stop killing them.

The thing I love about this book is its pre-empting of the escalating violence in computer games that dominates teenage children's lives today. *Only You Can Save Mankind* was released in 1992 and demonstrates the birth of the violent, gun-obsessed warfare games of the new millennium, although reference is also made to a violent gun movie of the 1970s, *Dirty Harry*, with the amended catch-phrase: 'Go ahead… make my stardate.'

Johnny and his friends are credible characters teetering on the outbreak of their teenage angst. They have endemic childhood problems, such as parents going through a divorce (known as 'trying times'), older and more reckless siblings, and a love of fast food and talking nonsense, but the nonsense leads somewhere, especially for Johnny. He has an extra layer of perception – he can see into things others can't – and his

---

The second Johnny Maxwell novel, *Johnny and the Dead*, was conceived before *Only You Can Save Mankind*, but Pratchett wanted to write *Mankind* first because he thought somebody else would do it.

friends accept that about him, enjoying the thrill of their adventures with him.

Perhaps the most important part of the book is when Bigmac escapes certain death after Johnny diverts him away from joy-riding a stolen car. The fright experienced by the boy is perfectly pitched and really brings home one of life's harsh lessons, especially when Bigmac sees his dead friends and is violently sick. He knows he would have been killed if Johnny hadn't arrived to steer him away from their influence, and therein lies an important life lesson for younger readers.

Despite his extra perception, we learn that outwardly Johnny Maxwell is just an average-looking lad. When he meets Kirsty (a highly competitive female), she remembers a chance meeting in a games shop with Johnny's friends but she doesn't remember him being with them. This is where Johnny teaches her some vital life lessons, such as you don't always have to be highly competitive, or shoot first and ask questions later. He teaches Kirsty that there is much to be respected in taking more of a back seat in life.

> "'... I've spent a week trying to Save Mankind in my sleep! It's always people like me that have to do stuff like that! It's always the people who aren't clever and who don't win things that have to get killed all the time! And you just hung around and watched!'"
>
> (*Only You Can Save Mankind*)

Only You Can Save Mankind is a book about growing up, seeing the truth behind the lie, or the consequences behind the action. Johnny and Kirsty are two extremes – she's probably too competitive while Johnny isn't competitive enough – but Johnny's laid-back style gives him the opportunity to see more deeply into the world around him. That's where his extra layer of perception comes from – he picks up the stone of life and takes a good look underneath. He doesn't just walk past it and ignore it, or not see it at all.

Johnny and the Dead is an extension of *Only You Can Save Mankind*. Johnny is now living with his mother and grandfather after the divorce of his parents, and it is here that he contemplates one of the biggest decisions of any adolescent's life: what is he to do when he grows up? He says that what he wants to be 'is something they haven't got a name for yet'. This is such a relevant explanation for Pratchett himself nowadays: a man who has changed direction in life because of the diagnosis of an illness and his confrontation of it.

'You can't just hang around waiting for great futures...'

(*Johnny and the Dead*)

So is there an element of the 12-year-old Terry Pratchett in Johnny Maxwell? Quite possibly. It is said that many great writers have a direct channel back to their youth, and by writing such credible teen novels Pratchett has clearly shown that. *Only You Can Save Mankind* was a good opening to the Maxwell trilogy but the next two novels were a considerable step up and explored important themes relevant to this book.

'"Never let superstition get in the way of rational thought..."'

(*Johnny and the Dead*)

With the second Johnny Maxwell novel having dead people as supporting characters, the inevitable question of what happens after death rears its head. Although this is not overplayed, it does provide a gentle pause for thought when one remembers the car-crash scene in *Only You Can Save Mankind*.

The basic story of *Johnny and the Dead* is Johnny learning that the local cemetery is being demolished to make way for a new development and the local residents (i.e. the spirits in the cemetery) don't like the idea and want to do something about it. Johnny can see the dead, his friends can't, and here the second Johnny Maxwell adventure begins.

Johnny is initially surprised that the dead don't look like something out of Michael Jackson's *Thriller* video – they're just former human beings with, mostly, not so out-of-date principles.

> "'... it is... very difficult to know that outside the game there's a room and outside the room there's a town and outside the town there's a country and outside the country there's a world and outside the world there's a billion trillion stars...'"
>
> (*Johnny and the Dead*)

Pratchett's ability to make the young appreciate the size of the universe is brilliantly simple, but this is the same way in which he makes them appreciate that the dead are not grotesque monsters wanting to eat your brains. They are former friends and family members; they are the predecessors of your neighbours, who were well known and not so well known; and they all lived and breathed and led full lives. It is thought-provoking to see how the different people in the cemetery met their fate. Some by accident, some through old age and some... well, that would be telling. There's a wonderful school project in the making here: researching the ordinary people of your village or town and finding out how they lived and what they did for a living.

Johnny and the Dead breaks down the stigma of death for younger readers and shows that life is a fragile place we all occupy for the blink of an eye. It also seeks an answer to the human desire to progress – indeed, is progress a necessity? Is it always a good thing? When large companies come into a local area, is it a good thing or a bad thing? Good for jobs and attracting people from other towns to your area, but what about the small local businesses that have been in the town for generations? Will they be swallowed up or go out of business as a consequence?

> "'Too much has been taken away... You dug up the High Street. It had a lot of small shops. People lived there. Now it's all walkways and plastic signs and people are afraid of it at night.'"
>
> *(Johnny and the Dead)*

There are so many different ideas and moral levels to *Johnny and the Dead*. It is an underrated book – the best in the Johnny Maxwell trilogy – and it is certainly the one book that should be on any primary school essential reading list.

Another firm school favourite is *Johnny and the Bomb*, the culmination of the Johnny Maxwell trilogy. Mrs Tachyon, a local eccentric encountered in *Johnny and the Dead*, is found semi-conscious in an alley by Johnny and his friends. The more time they spend with her, the more they realise she isn't as eccentric as they had initially thought and that she holds the key to different eras of the town's past.

One such time is the Blackbury Blitz of 1941. It is here, lost in their own local history, that Johnny and his friends learn some important lessons, because they witness the consequences of their actions when they come forwards in time again. What they thought they were doing for the best really wasn't. For example, if they try and stop a bomb from blowing up, different people will make different decisions in their lives and people who were due to meet and get married never will. And that's just a part of the changes caused.

Johnny and the Bomb allows children to look at their local area in a different way. To suddenly see their present-day, cosy surroundings as a dangerous place under attack from fighter planes and falling bombs, and to understand that things were once very different from the peacefulness they now enjoy.

At the same time, *Johnny and the Bomb* is a fun book. The interaction between the main characters is heart-warming in its strength and commitment.

It is a shame that Johnny and his friends didn't have any other adventures, because the stories, especially the second and third books, made children aware of local history and the consequences of their actions. Also, one would dearly like to know if Johnny's powers stayed with him throughout his life, and, indeed, what career path he would eventually follow (as the question was asked within the series). It would have been nice to see him grow up and continue his adventures and see how his friendships with Yo-less, Wobbler and Bigmac matured. And with Kirsty making a return in the third book, after helping Johnny save mankind in the first book, would a relationship blossom?

The Johnny Maxwell novels are about the chances and choices of youth, about being aware and focused and forever questioning and not taking things for granted. They are simply one of the best series of books in Pratchett's back catalogue and give us many insights into the way in which he looks in wonder at the world around him. He tells us that he doesn't think the human race has got religion right but he believes in the human soul and its ability to want to do its best and go on to better things. The Johnny Maxwell books also make us appreciate the things we have and the short amount of time we have to enjoy them. Our town will change, our friends will move away or simply move on, and people we know and love will pass away and become just a fond memory of a past life.

'Grandad and Johnny sat and looked at one another for a moment. There was no sound but the rain and the ticking of the mantelpiece clock.'

(*Johnny and the Bomb*)

CHAPTER FOURTEEN

Nation

'The fire crackled and sent smoke and steam up into
the darkness, and he saw them in the firelight, watching
him, smiling at him. He closed his eyes and tried to
force the clamouring memories away, into the dark.'

(Nation)

Sometimes authors who write a long series of books suddenly find
greater success with a one-off idea that has nothing to do with
their acclaimed characters and ongoing antics. A good example is
crime writer Ian Rankin, who wrote a short novel called *Doors
Open* that sold more than his last Inspector Rebus book.

This shouldn't be a shock. Sometimes people want to read a
specific author but don't want to start reading a series of books
from book number 19 and try to fathom what the intricate
relationships are all about. When one learns that there is a one-
off book, the desire to try out that writer is suddenly justified
and a whole new audience is achieved.

Nation (Doubleday, 2008) was Pratchett's first non-Discworld novel for more than ten years. It was a story that was just bursting to be told, and it instantly attracted much attention. It was a book both funny and sad. Again it featured a youth – a boy this time – on the verge of manhood and facing the complexities of life.

Before we meet the boy – Mau – there is a two-page prologue that reads like one of Kipling's *Just So Stories*, telling of the creation of the world in the story. The story itself is set in the 19th century somewhere in the multiverse – not our universe, but one where we can see many similarities. Mau is placed on Boy's Island, from where he is expected to make his way home within 30 days, leaving his boy soul behind in order to collect his adult soul on his return to the Nation.

After he has made his boat to make the return trip and has left his campsite spotlessly clean, he is overcome with anxiety. Birds explode into the air from all over the island and he collapses with the feeling that he should return home. And so he does, because only animals and boys flee – a man faces his danger. Then he sees a huge black tidal wave and becomes fearful of the plight of the Nation. Once he arrives back home and no one is there to meet him, he becomes terrified that a huge disaster has befallen his people, and cries the tears only boyhood can shed.

A key piece within the opening pages of *Nation* is the boy contemplating his vulnerability. He is between souls – boyhood soul and manhood soul – and that leaves him feeling exposed and lonely.

How many times have we seen this in a Pratchett novel? This is Mort, it is Queen Keli, Tiffany Aching, Eskarina Smith, or it could even be Johnny Maxwell. There are life rules in Pratchett's novels, and these are dictated by the age of a person. Children harbour the most pure but dormant magical powers, and they can harness them for good or ill and to varying degrees.

Children also meet disaster full on and get on with it. When Mau realises that a tsunami has wiped out the whole of his people and he sees the dead squashed in the remnants of his village, he blocks the disaster from his mind and buries the dead at sea so they can take on dolphin form (his religious belief). His mind wishes to replay the horror, especially at night, but he manages to shut it out, showing a maturity way beyond his age. Then the ancient voices of the grandfathers come to him, telling him that he needs to follow the tradition of his people and recite the final prayers over the dead. This is a most poignant scene, as the reader almost cries out: 'Hasn't the boy done enough?' The simple answer is no. He hasn't, and only then does the story begin to flow.

Pratchett had intended to write *Nation* before 2008, but the dreadful Indonesian tsunami thwarted that idea. There was no way that Pratchett could convince anyone that the book wasn't cashing in on the real-life catastrophe, but it wasn't. So he left it for a while, eventually releasing it after *Making Money*, his 36th Discworld novel.

The story of Mau, last survivor of the Nation, begins tragically, but he buries his dead at sea and he keeps his wits about him. For Mau, life has to go on, because he is the only future of the Nation. Very soon he meets a girl, Ermintrude (although she prefers the name Daphne), and, although they can't speak each other's language, they are of similar ages and brought together by the tragedy of the tsunami.

'They didn't know why these things were funny.
Sometimes you laugh because you've got no more room
for crying. Sometimes you laugh because table manners
on a beach are funny. And sometimes you laugh because
you're alive, when you really shouldn't be.'

(*Nation*)

Daphne is from the civilised world. She is a lady while Mau is little more than a savage, but the beautiful thing is that they both have their own magic. Natural magic, that is. Mau's is the ancient power of instinct and tradition, while Daphne's has been touched by science and the sensitivities of society. In short, he holds the old magic and she holds the new, and their relationship is forged from these opposite poles. But later Mau starts to question life and death and, of course, doesn't come up with any answers. Daphne's response to this is that magic is just a lazy way of saying 'I don't know' (i.e. it *must* be magic then). The layers of natural magic are again explored by Pratchett, which leads to the ultimate question: is there really any magic, any God? But all that is far too deep for *Nation*. The beauty of the story is its simplicity.

A canoe approaches the island and Mau stops it from capsizing. Inside is an old man, a priest from one of the other islands who has saved an unconscious woman and a baby. Now there are five of them, but the priest is scornful towards Mau, calling him 'demon boy' as though he has no justification to live while his nation died. Mau becomes incensed, hating the gods that have cursed him, but the old man, perhaps not unlike Pratchett himself, tells the boy that although his own legs click and his back aches, he finds a reason each day to be grateful that he is not dead. (A small portion of alcohol perhaps? Oh, the indulgences of the flesh!)

Nation could only have been written by a mature man, someone who has experienced the stages of growing up. It is a book that threatens to slide into cliché but somehow avoids them. Just when you think you know what is coming next, you don't.

Is *Nation* a typical Terry Pratchett novel? No, it isn't – it appears to be one of those books that a writer must write. Pratchett has said that most of the story came to him at once. It tackles Pratchett themes: the stages of life, the young having to grow up quickly, the big decisions in life, questioning God, old magic/new magic, and natural things that are sometimes mistaken for magic. There are ecological issues in *Nation* too (including global warming). *Nation* is a book that has tumbled out and touches on some of the darker issues that will appear in *I Shall Wear Midnight*. Perhaps because of his confrontation with Alzheimer's, Pratchett was suddenly facing bigger and darker issues full on in his fantasy novels, and not just in the Discworld books. *Nation* was a leap into the world of wider issues, and fans and critics alike instantly got it, making *Nation* perhaps the most important work Pratchett has ever written.

The story builds, becoming more intricate and more complex, especially when Mau's island takes on more guests: brothers, one supporting his very pregnant wife. But she isn't just pregnant, she is in labour, and this is where Daphne has to face her own personal demons. She remembers being a helpless nine-year-old when her mother screamed through her final labour pains and into death, for her and her baby.

It's at this stage of the book that Mau declares that he is 'fighting Death'. Note, not death, but Death, the Grim Reaper, the character so embroiled in the Discworld. And then with the knowledge of Discworld, we recognise that the grandfathers who speak in Mau's mind speak in capital letters. Is he mad? Is it really the ghosts of his forefathers? Or is it Death speaking to him? Suddenly the plot becomes even more involved, and the new woman gives birth.

Nation is about life and death, choices and chances, struggle and survival – finding out how little one can live and make do on. It's an interesting thing to contemplate in the material world we now live in – it's like a novel version of John Lennon's 'Imagine'.

Nation is a watershed in the work of Terry Pratchett. It is a book that serves as a reality check, a weighing up of all the wholesome things that life offers and can only be appreciated when stripped down to the bare essentials on a desert island. And then a greater understanding is born.

> **'Daphne thought: I'm learning things. I hope I find out soon what they are.'**
>
> *(Nation)*

Does *Nation* teach us anything? Probably not, but it does give us pause for thought. It allows us the opportunity to reassess what is important in our lives, as many great books do. All that said, is *Nation* for younger readers? If younger means teenage, then yes, but to give the impression that it's for ten-year-olds and younger children – grouping the book with the Bromeliad and Johnny Maxwell trilogies at the front of Pratchett's books – is wrong. A couple of milder swear words aren't the clincher here, it's the subject matter. The book is effectively about young people forced into a harsh adult reality, and that clearly doesn't work for Year 5 students and below. The children in the book are not children, they are on the cusp of their teenage lives, desperately trying to work out what adults with experience will do. Interestingly, once an older and wiser man turns up, we find Mau working against him, because he is now the chief, he is the Nation, and he takes the responsibility, not the wise old priest.

Is Mau in control? Perhaps not. Mau feels intimidated by the old man – the priest – and he confides his frustrations in one of the brothers. Mau is constantly asking questions at this stage, desperate to understand the ways of the shipwrecked girl and the adult things he would have been told on his return to the Nation had the tsunami not happened. Mau is proud but happy to concede his ignorance to the right person – someone he can confide in.

'"Look, I know you think there are no gods –"
"Perhaps they do exist. I want to know why they act as
if they don't – I want them to explain!"'

(*Nation*)

And like a good Discworld novel, the subject of religion crops
up, but only in the question everybody asks themselves when
something terrible happens: is there a God? And if so, why does
He let terrible things happen?

A time-honoured question it may be, and one often brought
up during the second half of the 20th century when discussing
the atrocities of Nazi Germany. Why did God let that happen?
Is it because there had to be a massive catastrophe for the human
race to stop and think that extra second to prevent something
even more terrible from happening? Perhaps. In the UK, it took
the terrible deaths at Hillsborough to shock the football world
into taking down the cages that penned fans in, and it was done
on the condition that a certain fraternity of football thugs
around the country would behave themselves – and strangely
they did, out of respect for the innocent dead.

Pilu (one of the brothers in *Nation*) cries. Mau knows that this
is the right thing to do, but he still doesn't manage to cry
himself. Every single one of his loved ones has been killed, along
with his way of life and his culture (some of its ways now
completely lost to him because he was never taught them). But
Mau responds to a responsibility, to protect what is left of his
world. How can he do that? By being there. Where he belongs.
Never leaving. To make his beer, to listen to the grandfathers, to
protect the Women's Place. Is that all life has to offer him? Is that
his destiny? Is that what being a man is all about?

Many men would be grateful for just that, but is Mau? The
future for him is loneliness if he chooses that path, because no
woman would surely want to stay with him in a den of shadows.

Mau becomes frustrated, and perhaps this is where we find Pratchett's true thoughts about religion:

> 'That's what the gods are! An answer that will do!
> Because there's food to be caught and babies to be born
> and life to be lived and so there is no time for big,
> complicated and worrying answers! Please give us a
> simple answer, so that we don't have to think, because if
> we think we might find answers that don't fit the way
> we want the world to be.'
>
> *(Nation)*

Mau challenges the old man about the existence of the gods. He asks why do people want gods? Surely people matter more? 'Without other people, we are nothing,' he reasons. But after only two weeks the Nation is a fading memory; people from other cultures are now populating the island and things are changing.

> 'He was here on this lonely shore and all he could
> think of was the silly questions that children ask... Why
> do things end? How do they start? Why do good people
> die? What do the gods do?'
>
> *(Nation)*

Mau knows that things cannot stand still and that he alone can't preserve the Nation, but he lacks the skill to give his plight direction. He believes the gods can't help him, so the answer has to come from within, but he can't do everything by himself. After a bout of much exertion and a lack of sleep, he collapses, finding himself at death's door.

It is around this point in the story that Daphne recalls the captain of her ill-fated ship reciting the Gospel of Mary

Magdalene at the funeral of a cabin boy. The interesting thing about this is that, in the real world, the pieces of papyrus that make up this ancient text were not canonised and are therefore not an official gospel, so this is Pratchett having some fun with religion again – specifically the Catholic church. However, he softens the blow by saying – via a footnote – that Daphne was quite sure that Jesus had a female disciple because somebody had to keep his white robes clean! Pratchett humour through and through.

The overall theme of the latter part of the book is the beauty of the uncivilised world. The Nation – like the most famous Native American tribes in antiquity – have their unspoilt history all around them. They have tradition and, above all, they have purpose because they have identity and kinship with their ancestors, or at least Mau does. But Daphne appreciates it too. She says that no civilised nation had ever visited Mau's island because the ancestors' gold and artifacts were still untouched in their ancient burial chamber. This clearly makes one think of the stripped-bare Valley of the Kings in Egypt.

Nation is not the culmination of many Pratchett ideas, but perhaps it is the most astonishing embodiment of them. His fascination with astronomy and the wonders of Mother Nature provides an interesting backdrop to a story about an ancient race destroyed by the powers of nature. Conversely, the primitive – surely not naïve – ways in which the natives act in *Nation* show a wholesome way of living forgotten by the so-called civilised world: 'If a lie will make us strong, a lie will be my weapon… People want lies to live by. They cry out for them…'

There is a trend to show the civilised world as the bad guys. A good example of this is the movie *Avatar*, but that was based on the extermination of the Native American Indian by settlers from the 'civilised' world and their trail of broken treaties – it's not a new thing. But something is surely endemically wrong with society if books and films need to remind the public of the splendour of the natural world and its people.

Pratchett talks of 'guns and flags', and this is a beautiful summing-up of the British Empire: flags being stuck in the ground of foreign lands and guns demanding that the flags stay in place. The fantasy of *Nation* – apart from being set in a parallel universe – is that the Nation actually gets something of value from the invading forces. Something the natives never got in reality.

> '*Thinking.* This book contains some. Whether you try it
> at home is up to you.'
>
> (Author's Note, *Nation*)

Nation (2008) and *I Shall Wear Midnight* (2010) are social comments about the society we have grown up in, about the bloodshed perpetrated by the winners (the flag-flyers) – the ones who write the history books and justify their crimes – and the rape of a nation's history by the gun.

CHAPTER FIFTEEN

Courtly Orangutans

'I have hugged an orangutan and worked liked hell to
get my hat out of trees afterwards.'

Terry Pratchett

In Malay, *orang* means 'person' and *utang* comes from Hutan,
which means 'forest', so orangutan means 'person of the forest'.
Orangutans are close relatives to humans but spend 90 per cent
of their time in trees eating fruit and leaves. They belong to two
distinct species: *Pongo pygmaeus* from Borneo and *Pongo abelii*
from Sumatra. Physically the two species look slightly different.
Sumatran orangutans have a narrower face and longer beard
than their Borneo cousins. Also, Borneo orangutans are slightly
darker than Sumatran ones.

Unlike many other primates, orangutans are not sociable,
especially not the male. They spend much of their time alone.
When a mother has her babies, they cling to the mother for a
while and then follow in her footsteps. They effectively stay with

her for the first five years of their life. If the mother has three young, that will be 15 years out of a life that lasts approximately 45 years. That is, if the orangutans live that long, since their natural habitat is in grave danger.

Indonesia has the world's third largest tropical forests. Unfortunately these forests are being destroyed at a rate of ten football pitches every minute. A report by the United Nations Environment Programme (UNEP) published in 2007 suggested that 98 per cent of Indonesia's natural rainforest could be destroyed by 2022. With only 54,000 of the Borneo orangutans left (rating them endangered) and just 6,600 Sumatran orangutans (rating them critically endangered), the future looks very bleak for orangutans.

Is there no hope for the orangutan? Is the world turning a blind eye to their plight? No, not quite. The Orangutan Foundation was founded in 1990* and Terry Pratchett is one of eight trustees dedicated to preserving the orangutan species in its own bio-environment and educating the indigenous people about the importance of the primates.

In 1995 Pratchett filmed a documentary in Borneo and London entitled *Terry Pratchett's Jungle Quest*, which showcased his love of orangutans and his deep understanding of their natural environment. It was a typically humorous Pratchett comment but *Jungle Quest* highlighted some big issues, which didn't go unnoticed. By the same token, it was a very heart-warming programme, with Pratchett having his hat removed several times by an inquisitive young orangutan and finding it impossible to get the desired photograph of an orangutan against a white cloth backdrop.

The Orangutan Foundation is the UK representative of the Sumatran Orangutan Conservation Project (SOCP). SOCP is a multifaceted programme tackling all aspects of the conservation of the critically endangered Sumatran orangutan (Pongo abelii). www.orangutan.org.uk

Pratchett's admiration for the primate was clear for all to see. As he took off his glasses after his hat was removed, he said: 'People with big brains and intense curiosity have always liked to poke their fingers into the electric light socket of the universe, play with the switch, and see what happens next.' He was referring to the orangutan hanging at his shoulder and it was clear that he enjoyed seeing one of his favourite creatures in its natural surroundings, despite the fact that he was plagued by bugs in the night and found himself wanting to destroy every insect known to mankind by morning!

The Channel 4 documentary was made in association with the Orangutan Foundation and also featured Ian Redmond, OBE, a tropical field biologist, and Dr Biruté Galdikas, who has studied the orangutans of Indonesia for almost 40 years. It did much to focus public attention on the unappreciated orangutan, Sir Alec Guinness writing in his diary 'the most impressive thing I've seen on the box this year', and many agreed with the great actor.

Pratchett became curious about orangutans after turning the librarian of the Unseen University in the Discworld series into one. Unfortunately – or fortunately, depending on which way you look at it – the librarian stayed that way. There were advantages in this. As an orangutan, the librarian is three times stronger than a human (some say seven times but Pratchett says three). His hands are bigger and stronger (very useful for handling large magical tomes) and his arms are longer than his body (seven feet when fully grown – what a reach to that book at the far right-hand side of the bookcase!). And, of course, he has a cracking ability to climb to the top shelves of a large bookcase, which has got to be a bonus (ask any student who locks themselves in a library). The downside is that an orangutan lives only half as long as a human and only says 'ook', which leaves them with very limited conversation (but does supply Pratchett's librarian with a bit of a catchphrase).

The orangutan of the Unseen University library doesn't have developed cheek pads, which so many female orangutans find attractive, but then again the sight of a female human, let alone a female orangutan, in the Unseen University is a rare thing indeed. Nobody remembers the librarian's name but it is rumoured that he could have been the quiet and unassuming Dr Horace Worblehat, although this is unconfirmed.

Pratchett has restored some sympathy for the orangutan in fantastical fiction. Poe had one as the mysterious foe in 'The Murders in the Rue Morgue', and then there was Doctor Zaius in *Planet of the Apes*, who wanted to hush up the past and kill all humans. So with that in mind, Pratchett is really blazing the way for orangutans in literature. He's breaking down the prejudices of authors past (it's suddenly equal rights for orangutans).

Although Pratchett makes light of the orangutan in his novels, in the real world he is deadly serious about them. He truly fears that orangutans will become extinct and that despite the efforts of the Orangutan Foundation, and of his many fans who raise money for it through their Discworld conventions, there will be little help in preserving the two species of orangutan for future generations. In the future, the orange soap-eaters (yes, they are partial to a bit of soap, which strangely doesn't hurt them) may *only* be found by our children's children in fantasy novels, which would be a great shame.

In mid-2011 Pratchett started to consider returning to Indonesia to catch up on the work of the Orangutan Foundation. In May he opened the SKYShades and Orangutan Foundation garden at the RHS Chelsea Flower Show, which combined his love of orangutans with his love of gardening. But returning to his fiction, the very fact that Pratchett creates a character in his novels (an orangutan in this case) and then pursues the reality behind it afterwards says something about his obsessive behaviour, or, at the very least, his inquisitive mind. He has truly embraced the endangered world of the orangutan and has made many members of the British general public aware of their plight too.

'Not many people get the chance to leave the human race while still alive, and he'd strenuously resisted all efforts since to turn him back. Since he was the only librarian in the universe who could pick up books with his feet, the University hadn't pressed the point.'

(*Eric*)

CHAPTER SIXTEEN

A Character Called Death

'Quantum physics is getting so weird the Angel Gabriel
could turn up at any moment.'

Terry Pratchett

Everybody who lives dies. That is a fact. Everybody who is
created in fiction lives forever. People around the world still
write to Sherlock Holmes and he is nearly 125 years old, so
there's the proof of that one.

Pratchett writes about Death as a character, just as his friend
Neil Gaiman does. But while Gaiman goes for a sexy young
gothic girl as Death, Pratchett sticks to the black-hooded
skeleton. Is he afraid of dying? 'I'm not afraid of death,' he says
flatly. 'What's there to be afraid of?'

'Is it all over, with nothing worse to look forward to now than weak tea, nourishing gruel, short, strengthening walks in the garden and possibly a brief platonic love affair with a ministering angel...'

(*Guards! Guards!*)

Despite an active imagination, Pratchett takes the great inevitable with a pinch of salt. He does say that he wants to go on writing, and you can't go on writing if you're dead. His philosophy nowadays – in the knowledge that he has Alzheimer's disease – is that he wants to stay alive long enough to finish the next book. But life and death have always fascinated Pratchett, especially death. It, or rather he (Death), has been an important character throughout the Discworld series (and even before it, see *Strata*). Just as in real life, he floats in and out of different characters' lives, cropping up and changing personal life stories – or ending them – when least expected.

Wizard Rincewind escaped death many times, but inevitably death comes at the end of everyone's life story. The only problem is the way in which one goes, a subject people try not to dwell on too much because it's morbid and you can do nothing about it. Pratchett, like so many people, is dedicated to making a difference while he is still here, entertaining people with tales of the Discworld, but he has vowed never to tie up all the threads of Discworld in one grand finale. He will allow the characters to live on in his books. The Discworld will not be destroyed, as once feared in *The Light Fantastic*. It will not be ended by a dreadful piece of magic from a renegade from the Unseen University.

This decision by Pratchett tells us much about his philosophy of life: that life goes on, maybe not your personal life, but the lives of your children and your children's children – or indeed other people's children – and you live on in their memories.

Cures to terminal illnesses will be found, a greater understanding of the universe and its building blocks will be reached and people will begin to live longer and longer due to medical advances (and the pensionable age will go up as a consequence). 'We are creatures of science,' Pratchett says, but qualifies that with: 'It controls us as much as we control it.'

> **'And this is the room where the future pours into the past via the pinch of the now.'**
>
> *(Reaper Man)*

The Grim Reaper, Death, the time-honoured skeleton with a scythe – although Pratchett has changed the look of everything and everyone else in his stories, good old Death remains the same.

Some people argue that if there is a Death there should be a God, thus confusing the Devil and Death, but Pratchett adopts an ancient philosophy by creating gods – very interesting for a man who doesn't believe in God. However, towards the end of *Reaper Man,* Death states: 'THERE IS NO HOPE BUT US. THERE IS NO MERCY BUT US. THERE IS NO JUSTICE. THERE IS JUST US.'

Through Death, Pratchett makes some important statements about life, death, the universe and religion. Like most other issues he touches upon in his books, he doesn't dwell on them, he highlights them, sometimes not even passing judgement but bringing them to the reader's mind so they can conjure with them. Again, in *Reaper Man* we read this: 'ALL THINGS THAT ARE, ARE OURS. BUT WE MUST CARE. FOR IF WE DO NOT CARE, WE DO NOT EXIST. IF WE DO NOT EXIST, THEN THERE IS NOTHING BUT BLIND OBLIVION.'

I find the above quote one of the most important in all of Terry Pratchett's work. It works on so many different levels. You could interpret it as a comment on how the human race harbours dangerous technology, or how it treats the environment. These are not leaps of faith. Don't forget that Pratchett worked for the nuclear industry and saw things there that surprised him to say the least. He is also concerned about the plight of the orangutan and its natural environment of the rain forest, so thoughts along these lines will pop into his head from time to time, as they do for many people. But another way to look at this, especially when said by the Grim Reaper himself, is: there is nothing but dark 'oblivion' after death.

The British Humanist Association is 'a national charity working on behalf of non-religious people who seek to live ethical and fulfilling lives on the basis of reason and humanity'. The Association claims that it is made up of atheists and agnostics. Pratchett is not an atheist, but he is a practitioner of 'the goals of human welfare', which define his everyday life.

> 'One Catholic couple with a baby boy... They were getting up early every Sunday morning to go to mass just as usual – but kids will talk. One Mormon family of the new schism – that's three more, and their kids. The rest are the usual run of Protestants and one atheist... that is, he thought he was an atheist, until Michael made him open his eyes. He came here to scoff; he stayed to learn.'
>
> Robert A Heinlein (*Stranger in a Strange Land*)

In April 2011, the general secretary of the British Humanist Association attended the National Union of Teachers (NUT) conference and was interested in the criticism that was made of faith schools for allegedly failing to promote tolerance and equality. The subject of how faith schools should behave is a complex issue and not one to be dealt with superficially. A faith school is shaped by its religion and therefore brings up children in accordance with the faith practised by its church and the teachers and parents associated with it, i.e. believers. To dilute that with children and teachers not prepared to follow the rules has one of two serious outcomes: a) the non-faith child fails to be stimulated by the doctrine of the school, or b) a sense of alienation and isolation will prevail through that child's school life because he/she and their parents don't understand or wish to embrace the faith that is all around them on a daily basis.

The British Humanist Association discusses and explores large and complex issues, and Pratchett and other celebrities and writers, such as Philip Pullman, very much support its culture. This is not to bring down other faiths and beliefs but to exercise their own thoughts and philosophy.

> 'I'm responsible, there is a meaning, and it is to make things better and to work for greater good and greater wisdom. That's my meaning.'
>
> Philip Pullman

This very grounded statement was made by Pullman on the British Humanist Association's website, and in a way it echoes the very core of Pratchett's determination. His inner strength really does come from an understanding of who he is and ownership of his own destiny. Both writers have much in common: not just their similar thoughts regarding religion but the expression of their thoughts, opinions and humour through the medium of fantasy. They are the perfect partnership for writing a great fantasy novel, with their witches and demons against the background of a form of religious power. Many wish for a revival of the Pratchett/Gaiman partnership, but Pratchett/Pullman would be so much more satirical, flamboyant and provocative. I am not criticising Gaiman: the sleek darkness he captures in his books is masterful, witness *Coraline*, a book nobody wanted to publish and everybody wanted rewritten. Gaiman stuck to his guns and a wonderfully Grimm-like tale was told, which transferred beautifully to the big screen. As we now enjoy a Pratchett/Gaiman tale in *Good Omens*, perhaps it's time to press for a Pratchett/Pullman one, and see how the great humanists collaborate.

Pullman made his feelings on Christianity known with the book *The Good Man Jesus and the Scoundrel Christ*. In 2010 both Pullman and Pratchett added their names to a public letter opposing the honour of a state visit to Britain by Pope Ratzinger. The reasons they – and like-minded people – gave for signing the letter was the Catholic church's stance on the use of condoms, especially in Third World countries and where HIV is rife, promoting segregated education, and opposing equal rights for gay, lesbian, bisexual and transgender people. Other notable people who signed the letter were Stephen Fry and Professor Richard Dawkins. The letter was published in the *Guardian* on 15 September 2010 and demonstrates the strength of opinion felt by Pratchett and his peers.

> 'He knew in the darkness of his heart's blood that he must not climb down. In the face of peril, in the presence of officialdom, age-old and vile, with its scarlet hands... he must cling to his dizzy crag until, trembling but triumphant... that as a creature of different clay he had not sold his birthright out of terror.'
>
> **Mervyn Peake (*Gormenghast*)**

Pratchett takes no comfort from God but believes that there is something out there that gives greater meaning to life, but he strongly feels that it will never be fully understood, or indeed ever be found. His early novel *Strata* suggested this and Death confirmed his resignation that he will never know. Indeed, there are so many mysteries overlooked or taken for granted in this world – and deep down in the darkest recesses of the planet's oceans – that no one is capable of understanding or piecing together the evolution or human history of the world.

In 2011 it was announced that NASA was assisting with the archaeological exploration of ancient Egypt. It was speculated that only 1 per cent of ancient Egypt had been discovered and it had been many years since a pyramid had been found. Scans from space showed much potential for new and exciting discoveries, but what would those discoveries prove? Clearly they had the potential to reshape the history books, but would they come any closer to the truth? And would the truth have anything to do with the birth of creation? Unlikely. But one thing is interesting and harks back to an amazing discovery made in Egypt in 1922: the tomb of Tutankhamun. There are top scholars who believe that papyrus was discovered that showed that Tutankhamun's father was actually Akhenaton (since proven by DNA tests), who was a follower of one God, destroying all other Egyptian gods, only for them to be reinstated after his death. It is then said that some of the events described in the papyrus are close to events detailed in the Old Testament, which led scholars to believe – or at least speculate – that Akhenaton was actually Moses and that the Bible was based on Egyptian history.

Unfortunately the papyrus supposedly found by Howard Carter and Lord Carnarvon in 1922 was never seen, let alone analysed by any expert of ancient texts, and the only record we have of it ever existing is a throwaway comment made by Carter in anger to a British official. But what is important to understand here is that people such as Terry Pratchett and Philip Pullman are convinced that the common perception of God is incorrect and, ultimately, who is to prove them wrong?

CRAIG CABELL

'Why this is hell, nor am I out of it:
Thinkest thou that I who saw the face of God,
And tasted the eternal joys of heaven,
Am I not tormented with ten thousand hells,
In being deprived of everlasting bliss?'

Christopher Marlowe (*Doctor Faustus*)

CHAPTER SEVENTEEN

Alzheimer's Disease

'I will, of course, be dead at some point, as will everybody else. For me, this maybe further off than you think – it's too soon to tell.'

Terry Pratchett

Alzheimer's disease was first identified by the German neurologist Alois Alzheimer in 1901. It is a disease affecting the brain. During the course of the disease 'plaques' and 'tangles' develop inside the brain, leading to the destruction of brain cells. Although some drugs can slow its progress, there is no known cure. Approximately 420,000 people suffer from Alzheimer's in Britain, but only 3.5 per cent of those people are aged under 65. Terry Pratchett was only 59 when he was diagnosed with the disease. 'I'm lucky in a sense. I have been diagnosed quite early on,' he says with what could be construed as an air of optimism.

Pratchett thought he had experienced a mild stroke after

having a brain scan. Two or three years earlier he had noticed that his typing skills had diminished slightly. At first he put it down to the onset of old age, but he decided to have some tests to make sure. Initially he passed a mental test, answering such basic questions as 'what day is it?' But after reassessment he was diagnosed in December 2007 with a rare form of Alzheimer's known as Posterior Cortical Atrophy (PCA). Pratchett describes the symptoms as a shrinkage of the back of the brain. He was quick to tell his publisher and many fans about his illness.

According to the Alzheimer's Society, PCA is a progressive degenerative condition where damage to brain cells is particularly focused at the back of the brain. The death of brain cells is accompanied by accumulation of toxic proteins, amyloid and tau, that form plaques and tangles in the same way as in typical Alzheimer's disease. PCA is a rare condition, although it is noted that it has gone unnoticed in the past.

Typical Alzheimer's disease is most commonly associated with deterioration in memory, followed by a gradual progressive decline in other cognitive functions including language, calculation, planning and perceptual skills. In contrast, individuals with PCA initially tend to have well-preserved memory but instead show a problem with vision due to the loss of the motor effects of the eye, and experience difficulties performing skilled movements and literacy skills.

The duration of the PCA condition is poorly understood. Some people live approximately the same length of time as individuals with typical Alzheimer's (on average ten to 12 years following the onset of symptoms), while others live longer. Pratchett says that if you're going to get Alzheimer's, his version – PCA – is the one to get, and he has not been outwardly depressed about it to his fans or in the media.

The author broke the news of his illness to his fans in

'Discworld News', available through Pratchett's websites, in the following way: 'Folks, I would have liked to keep this one quiet for a little while, but because of upcoming conventions and of course the need to keep my publisher informed, it seems to me unfair to withhold the news.

'I have been diagnosed with a very rare form of early onset Alzheimer's…'

Pratchett was upfront and honest about the disease to all those around him. When asked why he had decided to tell everyone, he replied: 'Why not? I haven't done anything wrong.'

On 13 June 2008 he appeared on *Frost Over the World*, when he told David Frost about his condition and how philosophical he was about it. He explained that he would carry on writing for as long as he could. As he wrote in 'Discworld News': 'All other things being equal, I expect to meet most current and, as far as possible, future commitments but will discuss things with various organisers.

'Frankly, I would prefer it if people kept things cheerful, because I think there's time for at least a few more books yet.'

After making a substantial donation to Alzheimer's Research UK in March 2008, $1 million (significantly more than £500,000), he became their patron, saying: 'I think it's something we can beat.'

These were bold words, but it wasn't Pratchett's only remit for becoming patron, as he explained: 'We should be aware that it is an illness, it's not some visitation from heaven… It's not something to be ashamed of. [You haven't got it] because you've done something wrong.'

Making people aware of the disease, taking away the stigma, is also part of Pratchett's quest. He explained that research was going in the right direction and that promising results were not too far away, but would a breakthrough occur in time to help him? He was – and is – optimistic. At the age of 60 Pratchett told the media that he was 'trying to be philosophical' about the disease and hoped that a means of combating his form of it could be found.

It was Pratchett's father who always told him to be philosophical about things, and the author has tried to do that, but he finds it very hard to do in the wee small hours of the morning when one feels at one's most vulnerable.

Between 2008 and 2010, the general public has seen a significant change in Pratchett's ability to speak in public. When he delivered his speech when he donated his $1 million, he coped well with notes in front of him, but two years later at Trinity College, Dublin, he found it too difficult and somebody else read out his speech, while he passed comment from the sidelines.

For a creative man like Pratchett, his illness can be seen on the computer screen in front of him. For somebody who had always enjoyed the process of writing from a very young age and who had studied to be a professional journalist, it is a terrible and life-changing frustration, but one he has faced with courage and determination, so this chapter is not a downbeat one.

Pratchett has kept fans and fellow sufferers – and their families – informed about the way in which the disease has been affecting him. His transparency on the subject is terrifying and heart-warming at the same time, but one cannot fail to be in awe of the man and the steps he has taken to make the general public more aware of this disease and its effects. He has explained to audiences that he could spell a difficult word but then forget how to spell an easy one. He would give an assured interview, but if he took his pullover off he might not be able to put it back on again. At Trinity College he made the audience laugh about a similar predicament with his Y-fronts. 'You need to know about my pants!' he declared, tackling a dreadful subject with humour.

It was while writing *Unseen Academicals* that Pratchett finally gave up the keyboard and used voice recognition software to dictate his books. His book *Nation* had recently done extremely well in the book charts and at the hands of the critics, and the constant encouragement of the fans was inspiring. Indeed, when he made his donation to Alzheimer's Research UK, an internet challenge was released called 'Match it for Pratchett', where an equal amount would be sought from fans as a donation to the cause. How can one be down with this type of support?

The Match it for Pratchett website encouraged people to dress as orangutans and swing from trees, and spread the word of the good cause on Facebook, Twitter and blogs – anything that could generate much-needed funds for the charity. The response was overwhelming, and still is. T-shirts were printed and books sold on eBay, among many other fundraising activities. It is not just the money raised that deserves praise; it's the humour of millions of fans and their dedication to Pratchett's cause and the way they embrace his interests.

> 'You couldn't say: It's not my fault. You couldn't say: It's not my responsibility.
> You could say: I will deal with this.'
>
> (*A Hat Full of Sky*)

CHAPTER EIGHTEEN

The Dark Red Wings of Misery

'When I was a journalist, people would die "after a long illness", and that illness was cancer. But when people started to call cancer by its real name, research began in real earnest, so I thought, I'm not going to lie in a hole somewhere... I hope to make quite a lot of noise.'

Terry Pratchett

On 17 April 2011, *The Sunday Times* ran an article about the actor Sir Patrick Stewart and his support of Dignity in Dying, 'an organisation that wants to change the law to allow people of sound mind to call it quits on life before the full horror of a terminal disease sets in'.

Although an extremely fit 70-year-old who embarks on a 40-minute run every day, Stewart became aware of the possibility of debilitating or terminal illness after being diagnosed with coronary heart disease five years previously. However, in 2009 he joined Dignity in Dying very quietly. It took them a few months to realise that this was Sir Patrick Stewart the Shakespearean actor and former captain of the USS *Enterprise* (*Star Trek: The Next Generation*), at which point they asked him to be a patron, along with Sir Terry Pratchett.

Pratchett was mentioned in the *Sunday Times* article and also took part in a BBC documentary, *Terry Pratchett: Choosing to Die,* which was screened on 13 June 2011. In it he visited a man called Peter who has chosen to die at Dignitas, an assisted-death clinic near Zurich. The documentary was slammed by charity Care Not Killing, which believed that the documentary may have shown the 'benefits of assisted death with very little redress'.

Even setting aside religious beliefs, there is strong opinion for and against assisted death, with people differentiating between those who have a terminal illness and those who have a debilitating illness. Pratchett put his views over very clearly during the programme, speaking directly to the camera away from the main film and the two people documented in it and their decisions to die at Dignitas. The second man, Andrew, was only 42 years old but had multiple sclerosis and had tried to commit suicide before going to Dignitas. Here was a man who had really made the decision to end his own life, despite the anxiety it would cause his mother.

I can only speak personally about the programme, because the debate about assisted death is far too big for this book. One could read the title – *Terry Pratchett: Choosing to Die* – as Sir Terry contemplating taking his own life because of his illness, and I think that that is partially true. He was facing his own demons and drawing his own conclusions, and the painful thing is that I believe he wasn't happy with the final conclusion. He said he would like to die out in the sunshine. He qualified this by saying that sometimes the sun shone in Switzerland, but this wasn't what his heart was telling him. It was telling him that he should be able to make the decision one fine English day, walk out into his beautiful garden and die with dignity.

Very early on in the documentary Pratchett asks: 'Is it possible for someone like me – or someone like you – to choose the way we die?' To me, there is a longing to know the answer to this question. I believe that he didn't like Dignitas. In his heart he didn't want to choose to die there, and the reason for that – again my personal belief – is that he believes he can change the law in Britain to help assisted death.

Another important part of the documentary, and probably the most personal part, was when Pratchett went to Belgium to meet the widow of the author Hugo Claus. She explained to him that her late husband had wanted to finish a book before taking his own life, but unfortunately he lacked the skill to do so because of his Alzheimer's. He had requested death by euthanasia, which is legal in Belgium, and chose death while drinking champagne and smoking cigarettes.

'Not being able to dictate any more, not being able to write any more. Not being able to communicate any more...'

Terry Pratchett (Terry Pratchett: Choosing to Die)

Directly after Pratchett's programme, Jeremy Paxman chaired a BBC *Newsnight* debate about the many different reasons for and against assisted death. The subject was way too vast for a 30-minute programme, and just as the debate started to heat up it had to be brought to an end. The Bishop of Exeter was concerned about the vulnerable, while the stance of the group Right to Die was a clear push towards a policy that would allow the terminally ill to die through assisted death. In a filmed interview shown throughout the programme, Pratchett told Paxman that he believed that it should be possible for somebody stricken with a fatal illness to choose, with medical help, assisted death.

Two years previously, in October 2008, Daniel James, a 23-year-old English rugby player who had been paralysed while playing his beloved sport, had travelled to Switzerland to take his own life. His parents accompanied him to Dignitas and told the press that their son had a 'right to die'. No charges were brought against them. Two months later, in December 2008, the Sky Real Lives channel had made front-page news by broadcasting footage of the assisted death of US citizen Craig Ewart at Dignitas. On 25 January 2009, Julie Walters starred in a BBC1 drama called *A Short Stay in Switzerland*. Its theme was assisted death, and the script centred around a doctor (Walters) who knows she faces a traumatic death and decides to take matters into her own hands. The programme was extremely moving and showcased a very important and controversial topic.★

'People didn't talk much about that sort of thing in those days. Suicide was against the law. Johnny had wondered why. It meant that if you missed, or the gas ran out, or the rope broke, you could get locked up in prison to show you that life was really very jolly and thoroughly worth living.'

(*Johnny and the Dead*)

With television making people aware of the facts of assisted deaths (not real-life euthanasia cases) and respected celebrities – indeed knights of the realm – openly defending the need for assisted suicides, the stigma began to break down around the

---

The drama was based on the true story of Anne Turner, a retired English doctor who took her own life in 2006 at Dignitas because she no longer could endure progressive supranuclear palsy, an incurable degenerative disease.

issue, just as it had years before when people suddenly needed to utter the word 'cancer' and take issue against it. 'As every true wizard knows,' Pratchett explains, 'once you name something, you begin to beat it.' And there we see the reality inside Pratchett's fantasy world coming through.

In 2011 Sir Terry Pratchett and Sir Patrick Stewart continued to be at the forefront of breaking down and analysing the need for assisted deaths. Their actions and words continued to make the public aware of the grim possibilities in their own future and encourage them to discuss those possibilities openly. 'The bug-bear is the term "suicide",' Pratchett says. 'It's the woman on the viaduct… [and] that is a world away from someone discussing with their family that their life should end at a certain point… with the help of a doctor.' Bug-bear or stigma? It's the understanding of the dilemma people find themselves in, the hopelessness. How many people have witnessed the last days of a loved one begging to die?

Pratchett believes that assisted death is a 'sensible' option if you are faced with a terrible illness. He discussed the deaths of his father and grandfather, 86 and 84 respectively, from cancer, and said that 90 is no longer an exceptional age to live to. He is resigned to the fact that his Alzheimer's has surfaced early, but still wishes to live as long as his father and grandfather did. There is scientific evidence to suggest that he could, but if the Alzheimer's becomes too much he would want to opt for the dignity of human life over the sanctity of human life, and surely that should be his decision.

'I have no fear of death whatsoever. I suspect that few do, what they all fear is what might happen in the years or months before death.'

Terry Pratchett ('Book World', *The Washington Post*,
1 October 2008)

This chapter and its predecessor have tackled two separate subjects, Alzheimer's disease and assisted deaths. Although separate subjects, one has led to the other as far as Pratchett is concerned. He has spoken openly on both issues, sharing his views and discussing what the government has done, or rather hasn't done, to support sufferers. He explains that there are as many sufferers from Alzheimer's as there are from cancer in the UK, but only a fraction of the money is put into Alzheimer's research. 'You hear of people surviving cancer,' Pratchett says, 'but I've never heard of anyone surviving Alzheimer's.'

Alzheimer's and assisted death are poignant subjects for Pratchett. He is a humanist and so, although he doesn't believe in God, he does believe in some kind of order to the universe, as hinted at in his science fiction novels. For Pratchett, this rubbishes the idea that one cannot take one's own life, because to him life is not a blessing from God. He explains that there is no solace for him in that idea, which one could argue violates his own human rights, or at the very least gives him no opportunity to exercise his own solution to his incurable illness when the plight becomes too much for him. This is just an extra frustration for the writer to endure.

So how does he deal with that? He explained that when he was diagnosed he felt quite alone medically. He then asked – through his website – for top brain surgeons and neurologists to approach him, and they did. These were people who had grown up reading his books and still enjoyed them, and now they were people at the top of their profession. Pratchett could use them as a sounding board for the jumbled mass of ideas and perceptions he had heard about Alzheimer's.

For example, it was said that mercury amalgam fillings in his teeth could have been a cause of the disease. He put this suggestion to the body of professionals – whom he nicknamed the Greek Chorus – but they were unconvinced. However, they did say that replacing all those fillings wouldn't do any harm, so Pratchett spent approximately £3,000 and had them all replaced. Afterwards he asked for two that he could make into cufflinks, but was told that they had to be disposed of as hazardous waste. He marvelled at the idea that he could walk into the dentist with them in his mouth but couldn't walk out again with them in his hand. He did offer to put them in his mouth and walk out the door, but the dentist was having none of that!

We conclude that Pratchett has a disease that is likely to kill him, that he cannot take his own life when the pain and suffering become too much, and the reason for that is the beautiful notion that God created life and we shouldn't take that away from ourselves. But if we did conclude that, we would know nothing about the spirit of Terry Pratchett – his optimism, his humour, his strength and his fight to make a difference.

Pratchett has used his imagination to make himself very rich and very famous, but he is asking people across the world (not just in the UK), through the worthy societies he now backs, to use their own imaginations (and apply some lateral thought) and change the way we deal with terminal illnesses. He is also asking the politicians to tackle radical subjects in a brave and pragmatic way – a shame, then, that as a rule politicians are not that brave and have very little imagination. But Pratchett will continue to break down the stigmas of Alzheimer's and assisted death, and educate people in order to change public perception. Once the public understands more, then more pressure can be applied to the powers that be to change policy and do something for terminally ill people.

'We are learning short cuts but there's always more that can be done.'

Terry Pratchett

CHAPTER NINETEEN

A Note About Cats

'Anyone who considers protocol unimportant has never dealt with a cat.'

Robert A Heinlein

It seems that with every passing year we lose some of the fun side of Terry Pratchett. Newspaper columns and TV shows debate his stance on assisted death and Alzheimer's, and because this is a vast and important set of issues to discuss, that's where we find Terry Pratchett's energy spent today and we empathise. Most Pratchett fans try to remain upbeat, so I decided to finish the main part of this book with a short chapter about one of Pratchett's most favourite things: cats.

Pratchett likes cats. They have been a major part of his household for over 35 years. In a 2011 article about a special attraction he was opening at the Chelsea Flower Show, the author is pictured humorously in his garden with a black cat, and that affection has translated into his work.

In February 2006 Pratchett told *Your Cat* magazine that his collection of cats was formed by accident (there were six at that time). The Pratchett family understands cats and their needs, and the author was quick to make this clear during the interview. He states that in his house there is always a bowl to be filled or a door to be opened. In conversation, Pratchett will explain that one of his cats, Genghis, will sit on your lap only if it fits in with his programme. Of course, this applies to all cats, and humans either like it or hate it – most love it!

Pratchett has an office cat called Patch, who sits in his drawer and lays back and stretches out his paws when he needs affection. Pratchett accidentally locked the cat in the drawer once, but Patch didn't seem to mind too much.

> 'Style. Beauty. Grace. That's what matters. If cats looked like frogs we'd realise what nasty, cruel little bastards they are.'
>
> (*Lords and Ladies*)

Cats feature heavily in two books in Pratchett's back catalogue – in one, perhaps, in a less serious way than in the other. *The Unadulterated Cat* (illustrated by Gray Jolliffe) is a stream of anecdotes that will please cat lovers everywhere, and perhaps amuse the not-so-cat-stricken too through its excellent artwork. The second book is *The Amazing Maurice and his Educated Rodents*, a Discworld title for younger readers. The plot of *The Amazing Maurice* is basically *The Pied Piper*. Maurice (a cat) leads a group of educated rats from town to town and stages a plague, which a human accomplice thwarts and they all get paid for. The rats ultimately want to live in harmony with human beings, but there is a fraternity of rodents who want to build their own super-race. The plot twists and turns and one can detect some big issues being raised, such as racism, discrimination and sectarianism. All that in a children's book, but again, it's there if you want to look for it – many people do, and discuss some of the nuances with their children as they grow up.

The Amazing Maurice and his Educated Rodents won the Carnegie Medal in 2001, providing Pratchett with his first major award. The book was dramatised for BBC Radio 4 in 2003, the character Dangerous Beans being voiced by David Tennant. It's a vastly different book in the Discworld series but still as ingenious and complex as his more adult titles. One could argue that you will like and appreciate the novel only if you like cats in the first place, but it has endeared itself to Discworld readers and has been a very popular title over the years.

> 'In ancient times cats were worshipped as gods; they have not forgotten this.'
>
> **Terry Pratchett**

Cats have an important place in history for certain races, and their influence is equally strong in the fantasy genre. Witness *Puss in Boots*, Kipling's 'The Cat That Walked by Himself' and the Cheshire Cat from *Alice's Adventures in Wonderland*. All of these felines are exceptionally smart and courageous. In the science fiction TV show *Red Dwarf*, the cat is slick and one step ahead of the rest of his crew mates. Unlike the orangutans we met earlier, cats get a good deal when it comes to their role in fiction. The reason for this is a simple one: there are many writers who like them.

> 'Cats have no sense of humour, they have terribly inflated egos, and they are very touchy.'
>
> **Robert A Heinlein** (*The Door into Summer*)

Pratchett on Screen

What follows is a guide to the major movies and TV series based on Terry Pratchett's work, including cast lists and short reviews of the features. On the whole, the movies based on Pratchett's work are well received. He also takes some part in them, tinkering with the script or having a Hitchcock-like cameo role.

TRUCKERS (TV)

Release date: 1992
Director: Jackie Cockle, Chris Taylor and Francis Vose
Screenplay: Brian Trueman

Cast:
Maskin (voice) Joe McGann, *Grimma (voice)* Debra Gillett, *Granma Morie/Baroness of Delicacy (voice)* Rosaline Williams, *Tom/Count of Hardware (voice)* John Jardine, *The Thing (voice)* Edward Kelsey, *Angelo (voice)* Nigel Carrington, *Duke (voice)*

David Scase, *Dorcas/additional voices (voice)* Brian Trueman, *The Abbot (voice)* Michael Hordern, *Gurder (voice)* Brian Southwood, *Vinto Pimmie/additional voices (voice)* Jimmy Hibbert.

Crew: *Producers* Brian Crossgrove, Mark Hall, *Music* Colin Towns, *Cinematography* Jerry Andrews, Mark Stewart, *Animation* Paul Berry, Paul Couvela, Andrea Lord, Lloyd Price, Sue Pugh, Stuart Sutcliffe.

Cosgrove Halls Films, Thames Television

A largely forgotten stop-motion animation, lovingly made but rarely seen. The voices are great and the animation extremely good too. A perfect Sunday morning film for children.

WYRD SISTERS (TV)
Release date: 1997
Produced and directed: Jean Flynn

Cast:
Death Christopher Lee, *Magrat* Jane Horrocks, *Nanny Ogg* June Whitfield, *Granny Weatherwax* Annette Crosbie, *Duchess Felmet* Eleanor Bron, *The Fool/Tomjon* Les Dennis, *Additional voices of unspecified characters* Andy Hockley, David Holt, Jimmy Hibbert, Rob Rackstraw, Melissa Sinden, Taff Girdlestone.

Crew:
Executive producer Mark Hall, *Associate producer for Carrington Productions International* Craig Hemmings, *Music* Keith Hopwood and Phil Bush, *Production manager* Laura Cosgrove, *Digital colour designers* Joan Jones, Jackie Mitchell, *Background designer/character designer* Steve Maher, *Background designers* John

Millington, Peter Hiller, Margaret Riley, Max Doig, *Animation director* John Offord, *Animator* Stewart Selkirk, *Animation character developers* Johnathan Webb, Alistair Fell, *Technical coordinator* Phil Atack, *Pre-production assistant* Nicola Davies, *Production assistant* Hilary Downs, *Production controller* Phil Slattery, *Animo special effects* Peter Kidd, *Silicon Graphics special effects* Colin Ralph, Storyboards.

Backgrounds, layouts: Cartoon Production SL and Milimetros SA
Audio post-production: Hullaballoo Studios
Digital picture edit: Flix Facilities
Title sequence: Editz

Perhaps the least impressive adaptation of a Pratchett novel. The story content is fine but the graphics look a little washed out and lack detail. Good for the younger viewers who, in fairness, are its target market, but not a classic by any stretch of the imagination.

SOUL MUSIC (TV)
Release date: 1997
Produced and directed: Jean Flynn

Cast:
Death (voice) Christopher Lee, *Mustrum Ridcully (voice)* Graham Crowden, *Impy y Celyn (voice)* Andy Hockley, *Mort (voice)* Neil Morrissey, *Asphalt (voice)* Bernard Wrigley, *Susan Sto Helit (voice)* Debra Gillett, *Albert (voice)* Bryan Pringle, *Voices for uncredited characters* Rosaline Scale, Jimmy Hibbert, Rob Rackstraw, George Harris, John Jardine, Maggie Fox, David Holt, Melissa Sinden.

Crew:

Executive producer Mark Hall, *Associate producer for Carrington Productions International* Craig Hemmings, *Music* Keith Hopwood, Phil Bush, *Production manager* Laura Crossgrove, *Storyboard artists* Andy James, Wayne Thomas, *Digital painters* Carla Abraham, Althea Deane, Marie Dembinski, Sue Halliwell, Christine Kershaw, *Digital compositors* Peter Kidd, Wendy Senior, *Scanner and digital colouring* Jackie Mitchell, Joan Jones, Jenni Roberts, *Silicon Graphic designer* Colin Ralph, *Assistant animators* Carla Abraham, David Aldred, Toni Andronlino, Les Brookshank, David Brown, Mike Coles, Althea Deane, Karen Heywood, Nicola Marlborough, Judy Pilsbury, Rhian Rushton, Bill Tapp, Don Walsh, *Key animators* Garry Andrews, Simon Bradbury, Robert Brown, Mark Burnell, Meryl Edge, Roy Evans, Chris Fenna, Claire Grey, Ken Hayes, Steve John, Mark Lewis, Les Orton, Garry Owen, Mike Price, Mair Thomas, *Layout artists* Sam Bailey, Tom Bailey, *Background designers* Max Doig, Peter Hiller, Steve Maher, John Millington, *Animation character developers* Alistair Fell, Jonathan Webb, *Background artists* Paul Harrison, Mike Hill, Graham Howells, Jimmy Lawlor, *Character designer* Steve Maher, *Animation coordinator* Roy Huckerby, *Technical coordinator* Phil Atack, *Pre-production assistant* Nicola Davies, *Production assistant* Hilary Downs, *Production controller* Phil Slattery.

Edited: Delixe
Length: 159 minutes

More rock music than soul music. An enjoyable romp through the Discworld. A little bit more boisterous than *Wyrd Sisters* but still a very enjoyable animated movie, especially for people not acquainted with the Discworld series.

JOHNNY AND THE BOMB (TV)

Release date: 2006
Director: Dermot Boyd
Screenplay: Peter Tabern

Cast:
Carol Maxwell Samantha Seager, *Mildred Seeley* Felicity
Montagu, *Home Guard* Ray Brandon, *PC Gallagher* Anthony
Bowers, *Mrs Tachyon* Zoe Wanamaker, *Bigmac* Scott Kay, *Yo-Less*
Lucien Laviscount, *Johnny Maxwell* George MacKay, *Wobbler*
Kyle Herbert, *Tom Maxwell* Frank Finlay, *Kirsty* Jazmine Franks,
Staff Nurse Sally Sheridan, *Rose Bushell* Holliday Granger, *Mrs
Wilkinson* Beatrice Kelley, *Councillor Seeley* John Henshaw, *Dr
Harris* William Beck, *Sgt Burke* Paul Copley, *Hickson* Howard
Gay, *Sir Walter* Keith Barron, *Stage Manager* John Axon, *Young
Tom Maxwell* Matthew Beard, *Old Man* David Williams, *Mrs
Bushell* Siobhan Finneran, *PC Collingwood* Patrick Connolly,
Lynn Partridge Maxine Burth, *Mrs Bushell* Eamon Riley.

Crew:
Line producer Anne Boyd, *Executive producer* John East, *Producer*
Peter Tabern, *Music* Debbie Wiseman, *Cinematography* Nick
Dance, *Film editing* Matthew Tabern, Jamie Trevill, *Casting*
Michelle Smith, Suzanne Smith, *Production design* Jason Carlin,
Art director Paul Drake, *Costume design* Jakki Winfield, *Make-up*
Sallie Adams, *First assistant director* Alexander Gibb, *Second
assistant director* Roger Thomas, *Construction manager* David
Feeney, *Production buyers* Debbie Moles, Rebecca Moles,
Property master Steve Parnell, *Sound trainee* Philip Clements,
Dialogue editor Miriam Ludbrook, *Sound assistant* Adam
Margetts, *Dialogue editor* Zak Melemendjian, *Dubbing assistant*
Emma Pegram, *Dubbing editor* Jeremy Price, *Dubbing mixer*
Andrew Stirk, *Sound recordist* Mervyn Gerrard, *Foley artist*

Philip Meehan, *Title design and digital effects* Martin Ashford, Leigh Wimpory, *Stunt performer* Michael Byrch, *Stunt coordinator* Trevor Steedman, *Focus puller* Andrew Barnwell, *Grip* Matthew Budd, *Best boy* Peter Marshall, *Cinematographer special effects* Ben Philpott, *Daily focus puller* Christopher J Reynolds, *Gaffer* Alex Scott, *Costume supervisor* John Dunn, *Online editor* Marc Eskenazi, *Post-production coordinator* Rebecca Nazareth, *Colourist* Jamie Wilkinson, *Location manager* Chris Hill, *Script supervisor* Jane Jackson, *Production accountant* Gill Lester, *Production coordinator* Rebecca Pope.

Childsplay Productions
BBC
Length: 120 minutes (three parts)

Johnny and the Bomb was the perfect book for BBC Children's TV. The screenplay blended action and historical fact to make an informative but captivating children's drama. The young actors involved played their parts well. They are not exhilarated at being transported back to the Blitz; they are scared. They became even more scared when they return to the present day and find that the 'good' they did back in the past has had huge repercussions. Like the book, the film works on many different levels and provides quality entertainment for young and old alike.

JOHNNY AND THE DEAD (TV)

Release date: 2006
Director: Gerald Fox
Screenplay: Gerald Fox, Lindsey Jenkins

Cast:

Johnny Maxwell Andrew Falvey, *Yo-Less* Jonathan Annan, *Big Mac* Paul Child, *Wobbler* Charlie Watts, *Wobbler* Joseph Watts, *Alderman* George Baker, *William 'Bill' Stickers* Brian Blessed, *Mrs Sylvia Liberty* Jane Lapotaire, *Antonio Vincenti* John Grillo, *Addison Fletcher* Geoffrey Whitehead, *Solomon Einstein* Harry Landis, *Boatman* Roy Ellis, *First Thug* Tony Westrope, *Second Thug* Shend, *Stanley 'Wrong Way' Roundway* Neil Morphew.

Crew:

Executive producer Melvyn Bragg, *Casting* Janie Frazer, *Art department* Terry Jones, *Casting assistant* Stephanie Dawes.

Another excellent interpretation of a Johnny Maxwell novel, with an excellent supporting cast including the humorous Brian Blessed. Because Pratchett always tries to be around a production, the interpretations of his books always seem to be worthwhile and complementary to his broader work, which is a rare thing.

HOGFATHER (TV)

Release date: 2006
Director: Vadim Jean
Adapted by: Vadim Jean

Cast:

Albert David Jason, *Teatime* Marc Warren, *Susan/Death of Rats* Michelle Dockery, *Lord Downey* David Warner, *Vernon Crumley* Tony Robinson, *Mr Sideney* Nigel Planer, *Medium Dave* Peter Guinness, *Banjo* Stephen Marcus, *Chickenwire* Craig Conway, *Bilious* Rhodri Meilir, *Violet* Sinead Matthews, *Death/Narrator (voice)* Ian Richardson, *Quoth the Raven (voice)* Neil Pearson, *Corporal Nobbs* Nicholas Tennant, *Constable Visit* Richard Katz, *Ponder Stibbons* Ed Coleman, *Mr Brown* Geoffrey Hutchings, *The Dean* John Franklyn-Robbins, *The Bursar* Roger Frost, *Lecturer in Recent Runes* Timothy Bateson, *Chair of Indefinite Studies* John Boswall, *Death* Marnix Van Den Broeke, *Ernie the Cart Driver* Arthur White, *Mr Gaiter* Robert Portal, *Mrs Gaiter* Deborah Winckles, *Twyla* Madeleine Rakic-Platt, *Gawain* Hugo Altman, *Tooth Fairy/Bogey Man* Bridget Turner, *Pixie Helper* Gregor Henderson-Begg, *Modo* Trevor Jones, *Student Wizard* James Mellor, *Bobble Hat Child* Martha Katz, *Bobble Hat Child's Mother* Rachel Edwards, *Grotto Hogfather* Dominic Borrelli, *Guest 1* Jon Ridgeon, *Hogfather* Shend, *Young Albert* Fox Jackson-Keen, *Slimazel the Bogeyman* Don Wetherhead, *Carter* John Cartier, *Toothguard 1* John Warman, *Toothguard 7* Tim Plester, *Auditor 1* Peter Holdway, *Auditor 2* Andre LaMotte, *Auditor 3* Adam Marvel, *Auditor 4* Andrew Swain, *Additional voices (voice)* Andy Robb, *Verruca Gnome/Hair Loss Fairy* Danny Da Costa, *Ma Lillywhite* Maggie McCarthy, *Small Boy* Aaron Barker, *Small Boy's Sister* Lydia Altman, *The Toymaker* Terry Pratchett, *Mustrum Ridcully* Joss Ackland, *Washerwoman (uncredited)* Diane Leach.

Crew:

Producer Rod Brown, *Line producer* Sean Glynn, *Executive producers* Robert Halmi Jr, Robert Halmi Sr, *Post-production producer* Shaun Nickless, *Executive producer* Elaine Pyke, *Producer* Ian Sharples, *Original music* David A Hughes, *Cinematography* Gavin Finney, Jan Pester, *Film editing* Joe McNally, *Casting* Emma Style, *Production design* Ricky Eyres, *Art direction* Michael Kelm, *Costume design* Jane Spicer, *Prosthetics technician* Kristyan Mallett, *Prosthetic make-up artist* Simon Webber, *Assistant director: second unit* Adam Coop, *Assistant director* Peter Freeman, *Additional third assistant director* Alex Kaye-Besley, *Second assistant director* Paul Morris, *Storyboard artists* Sav Akyuz, David Allcock, *Art department* Jo Sansom, *Hod painter* Adrian Start, *Props* Keith Stevenson, *Illustrator* Milena Zdravkovic, *Carpenter* John Allen, *Stand-by props* Stephen Conway, *Illustrator* Warren Flanagan, *Prop modeller* Simon Gosling, *Property master* Ray McNeill, *Construction manager* Brian Neighbour, *Stand-by props* Stuart Read, *Chargehand dressing prop* Mark Reynolds, *Sound re-recording mixer* Chris MacLean, *Foley artist* Nigel Manington, *Boom operator* Richard Miller, *Sound recordist* Henry Milliner, *Sound editor* Chris Southwell, *Sound trainee* Tom Turner, *Special effects technician* Alistair Anderson, *Special effects floor supervisor* Alexander Gunn, *Special effects senior technician* Jody Taylor, *Snow effects technicians* Oliver Guy-Watkins, David Johns, *Special effects contact lenses* Clive R Kay, *Special effects make-up* Paul McGuinness, *Snow effects floor supervisor* Martin 'Marty' McLaughlin, *Special effects supervisor* David Payne, *Snow technician* James Payton, *Prosthetic make-up artist* Robin Pritchard, *Digital compositors* Kamilla Bak, Reuben Barkataki, *Render wrangler* Amit Desai, *Render wrangler: MPC* Jonathan East, *Visual effects colourist* Max Horton, *Digital compositor: MPC* Viv Jim, *Senior animation supervisor* Stephen Jolley, *Matchmove artist* Owen Jones, *Matchmove artist: MPC* Peng Ke, *Character technical director* Angela Magrath, *Simulation technical director* Greg Massie, *Render wrangler: MPC* Alan McCabe, *Texture artist: MPC* David Basalla, *Data operative* Marlin McGlone, *Matte painter* Joseph McLamb, *Digital artist* Paul McWilliams, *Visual effects producer* Oliver Money, *Digital colourist* Rob Pizzey, *Digital compositor* Becky Porter, *Character technical director: MPC* Sagar Rathod, *Matchmove coordinator* Becky Roberts, *Roto/prep* Becky Roberts, *Digital compositor: MPC* James Russell, *Digital artist* Anthony Bloor, *Character technical director* Laurel A Smith, *Digital compositing supervisor* Kim Stevenson, *Digital compositor: MPC* Giuseppe Tagliavini, *Lead texture artist* Kim Taylor, *Matte painter* Kim Taylor, *Visual effects supervisor* Simon Thomas, *Visual effects coordinator* Shanaullah Umerji, *Digital artist* Daniel Walton, *Render wrangler: MPC* Chris Wilson, *Assistant digital resource manager: MPC* Oliver Winwood, *Digital artist* Joel Bodin, *Matchmove artist: MPC* Anna Yamazoe, *Systems: MPC (uncredited)* Martyn Drake, *Data operator (uncredited)* Dan Warder, *Animator* Steve James Brown, *Senior digital compositor* Loraine Cooper, *Visual effects assistant producer* Paula Da Costa, *Lighting supervisor* Christophe Damiano, *Roto/prep artist: MPC* Luan Davis, *Stunts* Andy Butcher, *Stunt coordinator* Abbi Collins, *Stunt performer* Paul Kennington, *Focus puller: 'B' camera* Mark Barrs, *Trainee grip* Emmet Cahill, *Camera operator: 'A' camera* Sean Savage, *Focus puller: 'A' camera and Steadicam* Iain Struthers, *Electrician* Thomas Thomas, *Video assist operator* David Toft, *Camera trainee: 'B' camera* Jaimz Williams, *Video assist: dailies (uncredited)* Peter Hodgson, *Electrician* Wailoon Chung, *Key grip* Pat Garrett, *Camera trainee* Brian Greenway, *Assistant camera* Alice Hobden, *Still photographer* Bill Kaye, *Camera operator* Vince McGahon, *Second camera assistant: 'B' camera, Second unit* Mark Nutkins, *Best boy floor* Terry Robb, *Daily costume assistant* Samantha Cousins, *Costume assistant* Marco de Magalhaes, *Costume assistant* Yvonne Duckett, *Costume supervisor* Louise

Egan, *Assistant costume designer* Amanda Keable, *Digital intermediate director of production* Matt Adams, *Senior digital film editor* Rob Gordon, *Digital intermediate manager* Paul Jones, *Assistant editor* Doug Newman, *Composer: additional music* Paul E Francis, *Runner driver* Lucy Eldridge, *Post-production accountant* Alex Chapman, *Key floor runner* Graham Cox, *Script supervisor* Amanda Lean, *Location manager* Helene Lenszner, *Assistant location manager* Amy McCombe, *Production secretary* Jessica Read, *Production accountant* Rachel Quigley Smith.

The Mob Film Company

Hogfather is a nicely made film but has had a little criticism from younger viewers, who find a death scene near the beginning of the film a little too unsettling for its PG label. Although the movie is aimed at a young audience, it will still attract younger children, and that's where Pratchett's work does receive some criticism: not all of it is suitable for the whole family. David Jason, Marc Warren, Michelle Dockery and Tony Robinson play their parts very well and it is nice to hear Ian Richardson, in one of his last appearances, as the voice of Death, and, of course, Pratchett himself as the Toymaker.

The beginning of the film is taken directly from the very start of the book. Beautifully narrated by Ian Richardson and with impressive graphics of the great turtle, elephants and Discworld, it really grabs the attention.

The important childhood nightmare scene-come-true is there in its entirety, interspersed with a *Christmas Carol*-like spiritual uneasiness from the vaults of the Guild of Assassins. There is a dark underlay to this interpretation of the Pratchett classic, which is as provocative as the original book. When Death takes over the mantle of the Hogfather to deliver all the children's presents by daytime, an endearing humour begins to surface.

Something I particularly like about *Hogfather* is the art direction. The black and ivory of everything is quite breathtaking, especially when a spurt of red is added.

A very good movie all round, with lots of visual imagery and eeriness.

Hogfather proved to be a hit with fans and inspired The Mob Film Company to follow up its success with the very first Discworld novel, *The Colour of Magic*, the following year.

THE COLOUR OF MAGIC (TV)
Release date: 2008
Director: Vadim Jean

Cast:
Rincewind David Jason, *Twoflower* Sean Astin, *Trymon* Tim Curry, *Patrician* Jeremy Irons, *Narrator (voice)* Brian Cox, *Galder Weatherwax* James Cosmo, *Death (voice)* Christopher Lee, *Ninereeds* Janet Suzman, *Cohen the Barbarian* David Bradley, *Arch Astronomer* Nigel Planer, *Broadman* Stephen Marcus, *Bethan* Laura Haddock, *Herrena* Liz May Brice, *Liessa* Karen David, *Picture Imp* Geoffrey Hutchings, *Death* Marnix Van Den Broeke, *Head Librarian* Nicholas Tennant, *Jiglad Wert* Michael Mears, *Lumuel Panter* Roger Ashton-Griffiths, *Ganmack Treehallett* Will Keen, *Greyhald Spold* Peter Copley, *Wizard Leader* Ian Puleston-Davies, *Narrowbolt* James Greene, *Ymor* Ian Burfield, *Rerpf* Arthur White, *Zlorf* Miles Richardson, *Luggage/Orangutan* Richard da Costa, *Third Rank Wizard/Spell 2/Kring* Andy Robb, *Master Launch Controller* Adam Ewan, *Astrozoologist 1/Rubble Rouser* Philip Philmar, *Astrozoologist 2* Terry Pratchett, *Dim Student* Thomas Morrison, *Brother of the Order of Midnight* Brian Hammond, *Blind Hugh* Paul M Meston, *Gancia* Christopher Willoughby, *Weems* Pia Mechler,

Barbarian Chieftan Shend, *Barbarian 1* Ray Newe, *Marchessa* Noma Dumezweni, *Big Star Man/Star Refugee* Joe Sims, *Book Burner Woman* Bridget Turner, *Lackjaw* Rusty Goffe, *Alchemist* Richard Woolfe, *Spell 1 (voice)* Eloise Joseph, *Townsfolk (uncredited)* Philippa Burt, *Stren Withel (uncredited)* Jason Daly, *Cripple Wa* Allin Kempthorne, *Magic Sword (voice)* James Perry.

Crew:
Production executive: Mob Film Company John Brocklehurst, *Producers* Rod Brown, Ian Sharples, *Executive producer: Fluid Pictures* Dave Throsell, *Executive producer: Sky* Sarah Conroy, *Line producer* Sean Glynn, *Executive producers: RHI* Robert Halmi Jr, Robert Halmi Sr, *Executive producer* David Jason, *Line producer: Canadian water unit* Allan Levine, *Post-production producer* Shaun Nickless, *Executive producer* Elaine Pyke, *Original music* Paul E Francis, David A Hughes, *Director of photography* Gavin Finney, *Film editing* Joe McNally, Liz Webber, *Casting* Emma Style, *Production design* Ricky Eyres, *Art direction* Mick Kelm, *Set decoration* Lee Gordon, *Costume design* Jane Spicer, *Make-up artist: dailies* Jessica Brooks, *Special effects prosthetics* Maria Cork, *Animatronic character designer* Neill Gorton, *Make-up artist: dailies* Jo Houtmeyers, *Make-up designer* Clare Juhasz, *Senior make-up artist* Kathy Kneller, *Make-up artist* Karon Mathers, *Senior make-up artist* Suzi Owen, *Make-up artist* Jacqueline Russon, *Production manager* Sophie Inman, *Unit manager* Ted Ladlow, *Post-production supervisor* Shaun Nickless, *First assistant director* Peter Freeman, *Third assistant director: second unit* Lou Hooper, *Third assistant director* Ian Hughes, *Second unit director* Chris Plevin, *First assistant director: second unit* Christian Rigg, *Second assistant director* Ben Sweet, *Additional third assistant director* George Taylor, *Carpenters* David Abbott, Simon Alderton, Daniel Byrne, Joe Cassar, *Stagehand* John Chamberlain, *Plasterer* Micky Chubbock, *Painter* Ben Crosby,

Stand-by props Jonathan Downing, *Stagehand* Clive Drinkall, *Art department assistant* Natalia Eyres, *Carpenter* Eddie Farrell, *Visual concept: RHI Entertainment* Warren Flanagan, *Storyboard artist* David Allcock, *Supervising props modelmaker* Simon Gosling, *Prop buyer* Claire Grainger, *Carpenters* Peter Grove, Les Hall, *Sculptor* Emma Hanson, *Dressing props* Shane Harford, *Painter* Bob Harper, *Plasterer* John Harris, *Carpenters* Garry Hayes, John Heayn, John Allen, *Painter* Kenneth Hopkins, *Props modelmaker* Greg Horswill, *Carpenter* Michael Houseman, *Plasterers* Michael Houseman, Simon Jacobs, *Art department assistant* Samantha Kelm, *Plasterer* Pat Laho, *Senior props modelmaker* Matt Lewis, *Stagehand* Steve Malin, *Prop buyer* Alex Marden, *Stagehand* Mark Bailey, *Prop modeller* Glenn Marsh, *Stagehand* John McNeil, *Props runner* Nathaniel McNeill, *Props master* Ray McNeill, *Props modelmaker* Duncan Mude, *Stagehand* Jim Muir, *Stagehand* Keith Muir, *Plasterer* Eric Nash, *Sculptor* Matthew Neave, *Carpenter* Alan Neighbour, *Plasterer assistant* Otis Bell, *Construction manager* Brian Neighbour, *Stagehand* Terry Newvell, *Carpenters* Paul Nott–Macaire, Barry O'Brien, John O'Connor, Robert Park, *Propmaking assistant* Marie Parsons, *Hod carpenter* Dave Pearce, *Carpenter* Steven Pearce, *Construction coordinator* Nancy Pert, *Painter* Perry Bell, *Prop storeman* Neill Poley, *Stand-by props* Darren Reynolds, *Stagehand* Robert Rice, *Props modelmaker* Stuart Richards, *Stand-by carpenter* Steve Rodgers, *Prop buyer* Rosie Rose, *Painters* Brian Shelley, Lee Shelley, *Plasterer* John Gary Spraggon, *Hod painter* Adrian Start, *Sculptor* Joel Belsham, *Supervising painter* Matthew Start, *Stand-by stagehand* Jim Statchini, *Carpenter* Gerry Stewart, *Plasterer* Keith Turner, *Set dresser* Louis Turner, *Dressing props* Paul Turner, *Senior props modelmaker* Paula Vine, *Plasterer* Barry White, *Visual concept: RHI Entertainment* Milena Zdravkovic, *Plasterer* Peter Black, *Carpenter* Dennis Bovington, *Foley editor* Stuart Bagshaw, *Foley recordist* Stuart Bagshaw, *Sound effects editor*

Mike Grimes, *Re-recording assistant* Kirsty Jellis, *Re-recording mixer* Dan Johnson, *Foley artist* Andrea King, *ADR recordist* Gareth Llewellyn, *Sound effects editor* Shaula Lumley, *Additional effects editor* Ben Meechan, *Boom operator* Richard Miller, *Sound recordist* Henry Milliner, *ADR mixer* Beauxregard Neylon, *Additional sound re-recording mixer* Howard Bargroff, *ADR editor* James Perry, *ADR recordist* James Perry, *Sound effects editor* Jeremy Price, *Dialogue editor* Matt Skelding, *Foley artist* Barnaby Smith, *Foley recordist* Barnaby Smith, *Foley artist* Jack Stew, *ADR recordist* Graeme Stoten, *Foley artist* Jason Swanscott, *ADR recordist* Paul Tirone, *QC engineer* Thom Berryman, *Sound technical coordinator* Dave Turner, *Transfer engineer* Thom Berryman, *Foley editor* Owen Bleasdale, *Foley recordist* Owen Bleasdale, *Sound project manager* Richard Conway, *Sound trainee* Lara Downie, *Supervising sound editor* Dan Green, *Special effects technician* Warwick Boole, *Special effects technician* James Dunn, *Special effects supervisor* Paul Dunn, *Special effects coordinator* Wilma Dunn, *Special effects technicians* Catherine Hart, Mark Howard, Russell Pritchett, *Prosthetics technician (uncredited)* Charlie Bluett, *Special effects floor supervisor (uncredited)* Luke Marcel, *CGI artist: Lola* Grahame Andrew, *Compositor: Mac Guff* Romain Arnoux, *Visual effects producer: Mac Guff* Arnauld Boulard, *Visual effects producer: The Moving Picture Company* Paul Branch, *Compositor: Mac Guff* Bertrand Breuze, *3D modeller: Mac Guff* Matthieu Buchaski, *Texture artist: Mac Guff* Myriam Catrin, *2D artist: Lola* James Cattell, *Visual effects supervisor: Mac Guff* Rodolphe Chabrier, *Effects animator: Mac Guff* Matthieu Chardonnet, *I/O management: Mac Guff* Marc Chauvet, *Texture artist: The Moving Picture Company* Rhys Claringbull, *Visual effects supervisor: Mac Guff* Romain Arnoux, *I/O management: Mac Guff* Yoann Copinet, *2D artist: Lola* Joe Cork, *Flame Compositor* Fabien Coupez, *3D modeller: Mac Guff* Olivier Dannhauer, *Compositor* Rupert Davies, *Compositor: Fluid Pictures*

Martin Davis, *I/O management: Mac Guff* Emmanuel
Desbordes, *Lighting and rendering: Mac Guff* Selim Draia, *Digital
compositor* Hasraf Dulull, *Matte painter: Mac Guff* Alain Duval,
Compositor: Fluid Pictures MJ Azzopardi, *Render wrangler: Mac
Guff* Thomas Foncelle, *Rendering: Mac Guff* Julien Forest, *CGI
artist: Lola* Siobhan Fowler, *Texture artist: The Moving Picture
Company* James Furlong, *CGI artist: Lola* Katrin Geilhausen,
Compositor: Fluid Pictures Vincent Goodsell, *3D modelling: MPC*
Andreas Graichen, *Effects animator: MPC* Liam Griffin,
Compositor: Fluid Pictures Dave Griffiths, *Visual effects producer:
Fluid Pictures* Meg Guidon, *3D modeller: Mac Guff* Julien Badoil,
Compositor: The Moving Picture Company Alex Harding, *2D
artist: Lola* Rob Harvey, *Compositor: Fluid Pictures* Steven
Hawken, *Animation: Mac Guff* Jean Hemez, *Lead Compositor:
The Moving Picture Company* Suzanne Jandu, *CGI artist: Fluid
Pictures* Tim Kilgour, *Matte painter: Mac Guff* Jean-Sebastien
Leroux, *2D artist: Lola* Kelly Lindsay, *Digital compositor* Kelly
Lindsay, *I/O management* Matt Lobato, *Lead compositor* Reuben
Barkataki, *Assistant visual effects editor* Matt Lobato, *Matchmove:
Mac Guff* Peregrine MacCafferty, *Visual effects producer: Lola*
Michelle Martin, *Compositor: The Moving Picture Company*
Alasdair McNeill, *Character animation: The Moving Picture
Company* Jorge Meurer, *Senior compositor* Humayun Mirza,
Animation: Mac Guff Laurent Pancaccini, *Rigging* Laurent
Pancaccini, *Lead compositor: Mac Guff* Benoit Philippon, *Visual
effects coordinator: Mac Guff* Emmanuelle Pianko, *On-set visual
effects supervision* Reuben Barkataki, *Lighting and rendering: Mac
Guff* Nicolas Renou, *CGI artist: Fluid Pictures* Adrian Russell,
Visual effects supervisor: Fluid Pictures Mike Shirra, *Flame artist:
Mac Guff* Patrick Siboni, *Compositor: Fluid Pictures* Sarah
Soulsby, *Concept artist* Kim Taylor, *Lead matte painter* Kim
Taylor, *Production visual effects supervisor* Simon Thomas, *Visual
effects producer* Simon Thomas, *Matte painter: Mac Guff* Anne-

Laure To, *CGI artist: Fluid Pictures* Howard Bell, *Rigging: Mac Guff* Patrice Vila, *Effects animator: Mac Guff* Pierre Villette, *Digital compositor* Paul Vorsman, *Digital effects artist* Imery Watson, *CGI artist: Fluid Pictures* Steve White, *CGI artist: Lola* Rhys Williams, *Conform editor* Andy Wood, *2D artist: Lola* Max Wright, *CGI artist: Fluid Pictures* Sam Wright, *CGI supervisor: Fluid Pictures* Adrian Wyer, *Effects animator: MPC* Ashley Bernes, *CGI artist: Lola* Tim Zaccheo, *Systems: MPC (uncredited)* Martyn Drake, *Visual effects supervisor: The Moving Picture Company* Anthony Bloor, *Horseman* Andy Butcher, *Stunt performer* Michael Byrch, *Stunt double: Sean Astin* Bradley Farmer, *Stunt rigger* Rob Hayns, *Stunt coordinators* Frank Henson, Mark Henson, *Stunt performer* Nick Hobbs, *Stunts* Stephanie Lelievre, *Stunt performer* Nick McKinless, *Stunt actor* James O'Dee, *Stunt performers* Dominic Preece, Vincent Wang, *Stunt double* Bruce Cain, *Stunt performer* Maxine Whittaker, *Stunt rigger (uncredited)* Kevin Lyons, *Stunt double* Nick Chopping, *Stunt performers* Nick Chopping, Rob Cooper, *Head stunt rigger* Robin Earle, *Stunt wire rigger* Robin Earle, *Stunt performer* Rick English, *Stunt double* Bradley Farmer, *Grip: dailies* David Armstrong, *Second assistant camera* Alfie Biddle, *Grip* David Draper, *Second assistant camera* Kate Filby, *Desk operator* Jamie Fletcher, *Electrician* Jamie Fletcher, *Second assistant camera: Snowdonia* James Foster, *Libra technician* Dave Freeth, *Grip trainee* Liam Garret, *Key grip* Pat Garrett, *Camera operator* Rodrigo Gutierrez, *Supervising rigger* Christopher Hawkins, *Crane grip* Ed Burge, *Electrician* Jon Hearn, *Stand-by electrical rigger* Gerry Higgins, *Video playback operator* Peter Hodgson, *Videomix operator: Canadian water unit* Keith Holding, *First assistant camera: second unit* Alex Howe, *Gaffer* Terry Hunt, *Still photographer* Bill Kaye, *Galaxy crane grip: Canadian water unit* Rick Leger, *Camera trainee: first unit* Philip Martin, *Aerial director of photography: Snowdonia* John Marzano, *Electricians* Dave

Campbell, Richard Mason, *Daily camera trainee* Glen Milner, *Daily grip trainee* Simon Muir, *Grip trainee* Ben Nicholls, *Rigger* Keith Perry, *First assistant camera: Snowdonia* Barney Piercy, *Director of photography: second unit* Chris Plevin, *Crane grip* George Powell, *Rigger* Greg Press, *First assistant camera* Miles Proudfoot, *Rigger* Ben Carey, *Best boy floor* Terry Robb, *Second assistant camera: Canadian water unit* Dana Rutledge, *Camera operator: main unit* Sean Savage, *Rigger* Dean Smith, *Camera trainee: second unit* Paul Snell, *Best boy grip* Brian Taylor, *Mega 3 remote head grip: Canadian water unit* Bernard Van Speyk, *First assistant camera: Canadian water unit* Brad Vos, *Riggers* Keith Carey, Stephen Casey, Steven Challis, *Rigging gaffer* Steve Cortie, *Second assistant camera: second unit* Barny Crocker, *Sewing assistant* Janna Bannon, *Armour costumer: Schmitthenner Armory* Brawn Barber, *Dye assistant* Sarah Hamza, *Milliner* Kate Humphreys, *Sewing assistant* Elizabeth Johnson, *Assistant costume designer* Amanda Keable, *Costume assistant stand-by* Alexa Koyuncuoglu, *Costumer* Catherine Lovett, *Deputy workroom supervisor* Cheryl Regan, *Stand-by costume assistant* David Wolfe, *Costume runner* Jeni Campbell, *Costume textile artist* Alex Carey, *Dyer* Alex Carey, *Workroom supervisor* Lorraine Cooksley, *Millinery trainee* Jessica Corlett, *Costume maker* Conchita Currie, *Costume supervisor* Louise Egan, *Sewing assistant* Rachel Farrimond, *Online editor* William Chetwynd, *DI assistant* Alex Gascoigne, *Producer: Pepper Post* Amanda Heatley, *Digital colorist* Kevin Horsewood, *Assistant editor* Laura Morrod, *Sales: Pepper Post* Martin Poultney, *Editorial trainee: FT2* Steven Waltham, *Supervising editor* Shane Warden, *Driver* Nick Goulden, *Unit driver* Ergun Halil, *Driver* Jon Hearn, *Driver: Snowdonia unit* Aneuryn Jones, *Driver: grip* Andy Livesley, *Driver* Darren Lysenko, *Driver: construction truck* Ian Shubrook, *Driver: SDJ* Laurence Turner, *Driver: SA* Francis Udell, *Daily production runner* Will Abbott, *Director's on-set PA* Saul Abraham, *Unit medic* Dylan Davies, *Trainee rigger* Clint Edwards, *Floor runner* Nick Goulden, *Production coordinator* Matt Grimwood, *Production secretary* Victoria Hair, *Safety crew: Snowdonia unit* Rachel Hamer, *Script consultant: RHI* Lynn Holst, *Key floor runner* Lou Hooper, *Runner* Joe Hornsey, *Safety crew: Snowdonia unit* Paul James, *Assistant location manager* Lee Alliston, *Safety: Snowdonia unit* Aneuryn Jones, *Double: Snowdonia unit* Dylan Jones, *Horse master: Snowdonia unit* Dylan Jones, *Double: Snowdonia unit* Paul Jones, *Production runner* Alexandra Lavis-Jordan, *Horse wrangler* John Kearney, *Assistant production accountant* Georgina Kelly, *Script consultant: Sky* Huw Kennair-Jones, *Production runner* Scott Kitson, *Script supervisor* Amanda Lean, *Head of Sky One Press* Chris Aylott, *Production accountant* Daniel Liddiard, *Floor runner* Darren Lysenko, *Titles* Dolores McGinley, *Double: Snowdonia unit* Penny Netherwood, *Runner/driver* Paul Rhodes, *Stand-in* Steve Ricard, *Double: Snowdonia unit* Trish Robertson, *Helicopter pilot: Snowdonia unit* Will Samuelson, *Production runner* Harvey Snelgrove, *Aerial operations manager* Andy Stephens, *Location assistant: Canadian water unit* Darren DJ Biro, *Double: Snowdonia unit* Vincent Todd, *Production coordinator* Kerri Trounce, *Location manager* Bill Twiston-Davies, *Helicopter safety op: Snowdonia unit* Michael Wright, *Location manager: Canadian water unit* Robin Brinsmead, *Pre-production accountant* Alex Chapman, *Local location manager: Snowdonia unit* Joel Cockrill, *Stand-in* Simon Cruise, *Script supervisor* Julie Daly-Wallman.

The Mob Film Company
Length: 189 minutes

After the success of *Hogfather*, The Mob Film Company took a stab at the very first Discworld novel. As it turned out, the resulting film was based on the first two novels in the series, blending *The Light Fantastic* with *The Colour of Magic*. With Pratchett firmly involved – and taking a cameo part again – the resulting script was a good one. The production was slick, and the main character of Rincewind was played by seasoned character actor David Jason, who had wanted the part for over ten years.

The movie clatters along at pace, taking in most of the fun of the novels and providing fans with a feature-length multicoloured fantasy adventure that can be loved by the whole family. The opening credits say that the production was 'mucked about by Terry Pratchett' and it seems all the better for it too.

Sean Astin plays Twoflower and the chemistry between Astin and Jason is excellent – and Luggage too. With a nice little cameo from veteran Christopher Lee as the voice of Death, *The Colour of Magic* is one of the very best Pratchett-related films.

GOING POSTAL (TV)
Release date: 2010
Director: Jon Jones
Screenplay: Richard Kurti, Bev Doyle

Cast:
Moist von Lipwig Richard Coyle, *Reacher Gilt* David Suchet, *Adora Belle Dearheart* Claire Foy, *Groat* Andrew Sachs, *Lord Vetinari* Charles Dance, *Ridcully* Timothy West, *Drumknott* Steve Pemberton, *Dave Pins* Paul Barber, *George Pony* John Henshaw, *Priest of Offler* Don Warrington, *Miss Cripslock* Tamsin Greig, *Crispin Horsefry* Madhav Sharma, *Mr Spools* Jimmy Yuill, *Stanley Howler* Ian Bonar, *Mr Pump (voice)* Nicholas Farrell, *Mr Pump* Marnix Van Den Broeke, *Mr Gryle* Adrian Schiller, *Trooper* Daniel Cerqueira, *Sergeant Angua* Ingrid Bolso Berdel, *Mad Al* Ben Crompton, *Sane Alex* Asif Khan, *Princess* Paula Lane, *Roger*

Alex Price, *Old Lady* Gabrielle Hamilton, *Postman* Terry
Pratchett, *John Dearheart* Tamas Mohai, *Sapphire* Anna Gyorgyi,
Undertaker Bela Szekely, *Shop Girl* Anna Erdos, *Parker* Matt
Devere, *Receptionist* Angela Eke, *Hobson* Mike Kelly, *Cashier*
Istvan Goz, *Maitre d'* Szabolcs Thuroczy, *Aggy* Richard Usher,
Farmer Gabor Atlasz, *Bank Clerk* Tamas Saghy.

Crew:
Executive producer Rod Brown, *Producer* Sue De Beauvoir, *Line
producer* Paul Frift, *Executive producer* Vadim Jean, *Executive
producer* Ian Sharples, *Original music* John Lunn, *Cinematography*
Gavin Finney, *Film editing* Alex Mackie, *Casting* Emma Style,
Veronika Vajasi, *Production design* Ricky Eyres, *Art director*
Monika Esztan, Ray McNeill, *Costume design* Charlotte
Holdich, *Make-up artist* Reka Gorgenyi, *Make-up and hair
designer* Lesley Lamont-Fisher, *Production manager* Katalin
Schulteisz, *Assistant production manager* Batizi Timea, *Unit
manager* Gabor Ujhazy, *First assistant director (second unit)*
Krisztina Barkoczy, *Assistant director runner* Julia Hargitay, *Second
assistant director* Tamas Lukacs, *Second assistant director* James
Manning, *Second assistant director* Szonja Szekerak, *Third assistant
director* Andras Szucs, *First assistant director* Lee Trevor, *Storyboard
artist* David Allcock, *Leadman* Istvan Balogh, *Set dec buyer*
Nimrod Hajdu, *Production buyer* Magdi Kondorosi, *Swing gang*
Mark Kun, *Illustrator* Kurt Van Der Basch, *Production sound mixer*
Tamas Csaba, *Foley editors* Simon Epstein, Marc Hope, *Sound
editor* Dan Johnson, *Sound assistant* Laszlo Kovacs, *Foley artist*
Claire Mahoney, *Sound effects editor* Jeremy Price, *Boom operator*
Peter Schulteisz, *Key creature effects artist* Ricardon Contreras,
Special effects supervisor Gabor Kiszelly, *Pyro supervisor* Gyula
Krasnyanszky, *Pyrotechnician* Laszlo Pinter, *Creature designer:
supervisor* Ivan Poharnok, *Pyrotechnician* Attila Varsanyi, *On-set
visual effects supervision* Reuben Barkataki, *Visual effects*

CRAIG CABELL

supervisor: Digital Apes Zoltan Benyo, *CG effects artist: Digital Apes* Ruszkai Kalman, *CG supervisor* Laszlo Mates, *Matte painter: Digital Apes* Tamas Mate, *Matte painter: Digital Apes* Agnes Nagy, *Compositor: Digital Apes* Papp Nikolett, *CG artist: Digital Apes* Peter Obornik, *Compositor: Digital Apes* Attila Polgar, *CG artist: Digital Apes* Horvath Peter, *Roto artist* Rosi Ruiz, *Visual effects producer: Digital Apes* Zoltan Szarvasi, *Digital compositor* Zoltan Bojtos, *Compositor: Digital Apes* Zoltan Szegedi, *Compositor: Digital Apes* Ria Tamok, *Production visual effects supervisor* Simon Thomas, *Technical director: Digital Apes* Gabor Toth, *Compositor: Digital Apes* Gergely Velki, *Compositor: Digital Apes* Vajda Balint, *Compositor: Digital Apes* Peter Farkas, *Visual effects coordinator* Adam Fiers, *Visual effects editor* Adam Fiers, *CG artist: Digital Apes* Daniel Forgacs, *Composite supervisor: Digital Apes* Pal Klemm, *Flame artist* Lajos Kondor, *Stunt double* Bela Kasi, *Stunts* Roland Kollarszky, *Stunt double: Richard Coyle* Czirjak Krisztian, *Stunts* Levente Lezsak, *Stunt performer* Tivadar Mike, *Stunt coordinator* Bela Unger, *Grip rigging best boy* Gabor Balda, *Rigging electrician* Csaba Bankhardt, *Focus puller* Gusztav Kirsch, *Key grip* Janos Kiss, *Dimmer board operator* Zoltan Lakatos, *Grip* Peter Pozsonyi, *Assistant camera* Kristof Pardanyi, *Camera operator* Marci Ragalyi, *Steadicam operator* Marci Ragalyi, *Dolly grip* Istvan Torok, *Focus puller* Gyorgy Vesztergombi, *HD assistant camera* Istvan Arvai, *Rigging gaffer* Attila Bilik, *Rigging electrician* Zoltan Bok, *Gaffer: Hungary* Zsolt Buti, *Gaffer* Brandon Evans, *Assistant camera* David Gerencser, *Focus puller* Tamas Janossa, *Grip* Robert Jasz, *Second assistant camera: 'A' camera* Gabor Kasza, *Costumes* Zsofia Federits, *Costume supervisor* Gabor Homonnay, *Costume PA* Gyozo Macsuga, *First assistant editor* Anya Dillon, *Assistant colourist* Tamara Juristovszky, *Second assistant editor* Noemi Mehrli, *Colourist* Adam Vándor, *Music scoring engineer* Paul Golding, *Transportation captain* Mihaly Gal, *Location manager* Rudolf

188

Andras, *DI line producer* Bori Bartucz, *Script editor* Merle
Nygate, *Health and safety adviser* Janos Papp, *Script supervisor*
Dora Simko, *DI workflow supervisor* Zoltan Virag, *Medical
coordinator* Gabor Xantus, *Production coordinator: UK* Victoria
Hair, *Assistant to production accountant* Aniko Hegedus, *Production
coordinator* Amy Horkay, *Assistant location manager* Krisztian
Kertai, *Location scout* Barnabas Kiraly, *Pre-production accountant*
Agnes Kun, *Script supervisor second unit* Lili Makk, *Assistant
production coordinator* Emese Matuz.

Production company: The Mob Film Company; Sky 1
Length: 185 minutes

Moist von Lipwig is a con man who has swindled millions of
dollars out of the banks of the Discworld. He is captured and
sentenced to death, but his execution is only staged when in fact
he has been spared to give him a chance of redemption. This
comes in the form of being offered the job of the Postmaster of
the Ankh-Morpork post office, not a job to be relished.

For many years the job of Postmaster has remained vacant and
the post not delivered, but von Lipwig has no option but to rise
to the challenge – and the dangers associated with it – and re-
introduce the postal service. To his credit he does rise to the
challenge. He also falls in love but discovers that he played a
monstrous role in his loved one's family history, which he could
not have foreseen at the time. He decides to break off their
relationship because of it, but the plot continues to twist and
turn to a satisfying conclusion.

The movie is about the right length and is as solidly
entertaining as it is visually stunning. The wit of Pratchett is
preserved, along with the more sinister moments in the
narrative. Claire Foy is brilliant as Adora Belle Dearheart, one
moment pompous and aloof (but also sexy and alluring) and the

next wretched and broken. Richard Coyle is also extremely good. Some of the supporting roles are also played particularly well, for example by Andrew Sachs and Paul Barber. In all, it's an excellent interpretation of Pratchett's novel, with another great cameo from the man himself.

ANNEX B

Pratchett at the Theatre

'Terry writes very good dialogue. Not all authors do.
But Terry, like Dickens, writes stuff which you can lift
straight into your play.'
                    Stephen Briggs (Introduction, *Mort – The Play*)

It was not my intention to list every Discworld theatrical adaptation, because although they are based on Pratchett's work, technically they are not by him. This short annex broadly highlights the adaptations and the driving forces behind them.

Stephen Briggs is linked to Pratchett through his love of the theatre. Born in 1951, he is a civil servant who dabbles in amateur dramatics. His dabbling with Pratchett's work started back in 1991 when he adapted the author's Shakespearian spoof *Wyrd Sisters* for the Studio Theatre Club of Abingdon, Oxfordshire, with permission from the author. His passion for all things theatrical inspired him to take on the role of Duke Felmet in the production.

Wyrd Sisters was both enjoyable and successful, so the

following year Briggs adapted *Mort* and played the part of Death. This started a trend, as Briggs then starred as Lord Vetinari in *Guards! Guards!* in 1993.

Briggs has forged an enviable reputation with fans of the Discworld series and has gone on to turn many other books in the series into successful theatrical adaptations. He is so successful that he is even given manuscripts of Pratchett books in advance so the theatrical production can coincide with the book's release. The Studio Theatre Club is now a staple part of the celebration of Discworld and attracts much attention.

What is quite amazing is that the Studio Theatre Club was the first company ever to dramatise Discworld. Their theatre holds fewer than 100 people and has a tiny stage, but from these modest beginnings greater things were achieved.

Aside from the plays, Briggs has contributed to other works of Pratchett's (see Annex C). In his own words, he has 'been drawn further into the Discworld universe'. He was the driving force behind *The Streets of Ankh-Morpork: The first Discworld Map* (painted by Stephen Player in 1993), *The Discworld Map: A Tourist Guide to Lancre* and *Death's Domain*. His database also became part of *The Discworld Companion*.

Although other theatre groups have gone on to interpret Pratchett's novels in different ways, Stephen Briggs' adaptations are considered to be the benchmark and he is somebody Pratchett trusts implicitly.

'Death even got an invitation to London's flashiest Indian restaurant to have a curry with a group of journalists as part of the publicity for a Discworld computer game. A whole room full of journalists but, unfortunately for Death, no take-away.'

Stephen Briggs, reminiscing about being Death
(Introduction, *Mort – The Play*)

ANNEX C

Terry Pratchett: Complete UK Bibliography and Collector's Guide

What follows is a book collector's guide to the work of Terry Pratchett. It is by no means exhaustive. It concentrates on the main works available in the UK and their variants, so fans and collectors can tell at a glance if what they possess, or wish to possess, is collectable or not.

The problem with collecting popular books in the fantasy genre is that fans welcome limited editions, different wrappers, slipcases, signed and numbered copies. Terry Pratchett falls shamelessly into that category, so much so that I have not differentiated between uniform sets of his books, i.e. I haven't split this listing into first editions, proof copies, numbered and signed copies, etc. Instead I felt it was important to list as many different UK versions of each individual book as possible, especially for the early editions. That way it is very easy to see how many versions of *The Colour of Magic* or *The Light Fantastic* are available. I believe this approach makes the guide much more user-friendly and helps the reader avoid buying a version of a book that is very similar to the first edition and, consequently, save him or her some money.★ I feel this is a very important point nowadays, with many amateur 'book dealers' out there wishing to make money for themselves or some well-meaning cause. Suffice to say, only the first UK priced stickered copy of *The Colour of Magic* (for example) is worth thousands of pounds. Personally, I would not pay three figures (let alone four figures) for any other copy, but that's my own personal opinion. Conversely, I do not list every reissue of a book, as they are clearly of no value. The only book club issues listed are those for the early titles or 'The Unseen Library' editions. As a rule, BCA, GP and Science Fiction Book Club issues have very little collectability. Within the book-collecting world, first hardback editions are the most collectable, followed by limited edition copies and then proof copies.

The following guide is not priced because prices will vary during the shelf life of this book. I list everything in release order, but with the first edition listed before any proof copy. I do this because priority is given to the true first UK edition, which, although it may not be the most limited version, will be the most desirable, especially if it is 'flat signed' (not dedicated to anyone) by the author. That brings me on to my last point. Copies of Pratchett's books are worth more flat signed. Unless someone shares the same name as the person to whom the book was dedicated, personally signed copies are less valuable. The exception to this is an antique book where a dedication from, say, Bram Stoker may add interest (and maybe provenance) to a copy of *Dracula*. Nowadays, what with official signing sessions all over the country and writers being very generous in signing

---

There is some very slight repetition with regard to omnibus editions, to clarify whether a certain book identified in the bibliography has been included in a specific collection.

their older books (not just the latest release), people are prepared to wait and be choosy about the copy of a book they want to buy on the second-hand market.

As a rule, the book must not be price-clipped, should show its original price, have a bright and clean dustwrapper with no sunning or creases or tears, and preferably be flat signed by the author. Collectors don't ask for much really, do they? Also, nowadays, Pratchett has an official stamp endorsing his signature as genuine, and these copies carry greater authority. The first officially stamped autographed copies of a book I ever saw were of Christopher Lee's *Lord of Misrule*, the third incarnation of his autobiography; officially stamped copies are worth more than flat signed copies of the previous version of his autobiography, even though the dustwrapper was much more striking.

Note: The first stories of Pratchett's that had a public airing were those he wrote for his school magazine, *Technical Cygnet*. His first officially published short story, 'The Hades Business', was printed in 1961, and other stories are likely to exist. Two titles certainly do: 'Solution' and 'Picture'.

SHORT STORIES FOR THE *BUCKS FREE PRESS*

The following list gives precise dates and the number of episodes for each of Pratchett's stories in the *Bucks Free Press*. None of these stories were written under Pratchett's real name; he used the pseudonym of Uncle Jim. None of the stories were named at the time but they have been given titles since. They are not named here, to reflect their original state. Original copies of the *Bucks Free Press* featuring Pratchett's Uncle Jim stories are extremely collectable today.

8 October – 23 December 1965 (12 episodes)

31 December 1965 – 7 January 1966 (two episodes)

14 January – 28 January 1966 (three episodes)

4 February 1966 (one episode)

11 February 1966 (one episode)

18 February 1966 (one episode)

25 February 1966 (one episode)

4 March 1966 (one episode)

11 March – 18 March 1966 (two episodes)

25 March – 8 April 1966 (three episodes)

15 April – 29 April 1966 (three episodes)

6 May – 20 May 1966 (three episodes)

27 May – 15 July 1966 (eight episodes)

22 July – 5 August 1966 (three episodes)

12 August – 26 August 1966 (three episodes)

2 September – 23 September 1966 (four episodes)

30 September – 28 October 1966 (five episodes)

4 November – 9 December 1966 (six episodes)

16 December – 30 December 1966 (three episodes)

6 January – 13 January 1967 (two episodes)

20 January – 3 March 1967 (three episodes)

10 March – 23 March 1967 (three episodes)

31 March – 9 June 1967 (11 episodes)

16 June 1967 (one episode)

23 June – 7 July 1967 (three episodes)

14 July – 21 July 1967 (two episodes)

28 July 1967 (one episode)

4 August – 25 August 1967 (four episodes)

1 September – 15 September 1967 (three episodes)

22 September – 29 September 1967 (two episodes)

6 October – 27 October 1967 (four episodes)

3 November – 10 November 1967 (two episodes)

17 November – 8 December 1967 (four episodes)

15 December – 22 December 1967 (two episodes)

29 December 1967 – 12 January 1968 (three episodes)

19 January – 9 February 1968 (four episodes)
16 February – 8 March 1968 (four episodes)
15 March – 29 March 1968 (three episodes)
5 April – 19 April 1968 (three episodes)
26 April – 17 May 1968 (three episodes)
24 May – 12 June 1968 (eight episodes)

From this point Pratchett started to illustrate his stories

19 July – 16 August 1968 (five episodes)
23 August – 6 September 1968 (three episodes)
13 September – 20 September 1968 (two episodes)
27 September – 8 November 1968 (seven episodes)
15 November – 29 November 1968 (three episodes)
6 December – 20 December 1968 (three episodes)
28 December 1968 (one episode)
3 January – 17 January 1969 (three episodes)
24 January – 7 February 1969 (three episodes)
14 February – 28 February 1969 (three episodes)
7 March – 28 March 1969 (four episodes)
3 April 1969 (one episode)
11 April – 18 April 1969 (two episodes)
25 April – 16 May 1969 (four episodes)
23 May – 6 June 1969 (three episodes)
13 June – 11 July 1969 (five episodes)
18 July – 1 August 1969 (three episodes)
8 August – 29 August 1969 (four episodes)
5 September – 24 October 1969 (eight episodes)
31 October – 5 December 1969 (six episodes)
12 December – 24 December 1969 (three episodes)
2 January – 23 January 1970 (four episodes)
30 January – 20 February 1970 (four episodes)
27 February – 13 March 1970 (three episodes)

20 March – 24 April 1970 (six episodes)
1 May – 29 May 1970 (five episodes)
12 June – 17 July 1970 (six episodes)
24 July – 14 August 1970 (three episodes)
21 August – 18 September 1970 (five episodes)

EARLY WORKS – SHORT STORIES

'The Hades Business', *Science Fantasy* magazine, Volume 20, No 60 (August 1963), paperback as issued.

'The Hades Business', *The Unfriendly Future*, edited by Tom Boardman (Four Square, 1965), paperback as issued.

'Night Dweller', *New Worlds* (Compact SF, November 1965, cover story 'The Wrecks of Time' by James Colvin), paperback.

From 12 June 1973 to 4 March 1975, Pratchett drew cartoons for 'Warlock Hall', *The Psychic Researcher and Spiritualist Gazette,* published by Colin Smythe. Roughly 17 different issues exist.

'And Mind the Monoliths', *Bath and West Evening Chronicle*, 3 April 1978.

EARLY WORKS – NOVELS

The Carpet People (Colin Smythe, 1971). First UK hardback edition in priced dustwrapper (illustrated by Terry Pratchett) at £1.90, illustrated by the author. Mottled green cloth. 3,000 copies printed, most going to libraries.

Note: There are at least two copies of *The Carpet People* with illustrations hand-coloured by Pratchett throughout, and possibly another four copies with a couple of illustrations coloured by the author.

The Dark Side of the Sun (Colin Smythe, 1976). First UK

hardback edition with priced dustwrapper (illustrated by Terry Pratchett) at £2.50. Vermillion cloth boards with gilt titles. 900 copies printed.

Strata (Colin Smythe, 1981). First UK hardback edition in price-stickered dustwrapper at £5.95. Dark green boards with gilt titles. 1,001 copies printed.

Strata (Doubleday, 1994). First thus. Limited edition of 500 numbered copies. Josh Kirby dustwrapper.

THE DISCWORLD SERIES

Note: The Discworld series is listed in its official order.

Discworld 1 – The Colour of Magic

The Colour of Magic (Colin Smythe, 1983). First UK hardback with price sticker to front inner flap of dustwrapper at £7.95. Full number line on copyright page. 506 copies only. Pale green patterned cloth with gilt lettering. Note i: Later issues had reviews on inner flap of jacket. Note ii: The first issue of *The Colour of Magic* ran to 206 pages. The American Science Fiction Book Club reset book in 1984; this edition ran to 184 pages. It also had Book Club Edition on front jacket flap and 06199 on back of dustwrapper.

The Colour of Magic (St Martin's Press, 1983). UK export copy with $11.95 sticker on inner flap of dustwrapper.

The Colour of Magic (Colin Smythe, 1989). New UK edition with introduction by Terry Pratchett.

The Colour of Magic illustrated edition adapted by Steven Rockwell (Corgi, 1993). Paperback in laminated boards.

The Colour of Magic (Isis, 1994). UK large print hardback (also issued in paperback). Restricted to 400 copies only.

The Colour of Magic (Victor Gollancz, 1995). UK compact

edition (one of four compact editions released; all four also available in a slipcase).

The Colour of Magic released as *The First Discworld Novels* (Colin Smythe, 1999). Omnibus edition of *The Colour of Magic* and *The Light Fantastic*. Issued in price-stickered dustwrapper.

The Colour of Magic (BCA, 2001). Unseen Library edition. Deluxe half-leatherette edition with silk ribbon marker. Restricted to 7,000 copies.

The Colour of Magic (Doubleday and Colin Smythe, 2004). Twenty-first anniversary edition. Issued by Corgi for Ottakars: 1,000 special signed, slipcased copies of *The Colour of Magic*, together with a 'Discworld Starter Pack' – a slipcase containing paperbacks of *The Colour of Magic*, *The Light Fantastic* and *Equal Rites*. Note: Copies are officially stamped on signed page.

The Colour of Magic (Hill House Publishers, 2006). Facsimile edition. Hardback issued with two different covers: the original 1983 version and the 1989 version.

The Colour of Magic & The Light Fantastic (Doubleday, 2008). The Discworld Graphic Novels, with pictorial laminated boards and full number line down to '1' on copyright page. Note: For Christmas 1989, Corgi issued the first three Discworld volumes in a slipcase.

Discworld 2 – The Light Fantastic

The Light Fantastic (Colin Smythe, 1986). UK hardback with priced sticker of £8.95 on unpriced but unclipped dustwrapper. Blue boards with gilt titles.1,034 copies printed. Note i: Some copies exist with a review slip, as do all Colin Smythe first editions. Note ii: The 1987 reissue of *The Light Fantastic* was also released with the original dustwrapper (its own has reviews on the back, so it's easy to tell the difference).

The Light Fantastic (Colin Smythe, 1986). Proof copy with

dustwrapper (three copies apparently exist).

The Light Fantastic (Corgi, 1993). Illustrated edition adapted by Steven Rockwell. Paperback in laminated boards.

The Light Fantastic (Victor Gollancz, 1995). UK compact edition (one of four compact editions released; all four available in a slipcase).

The Light Fantastic (BCA, 2001). Unseen Library edition. Deluxe half-leatherette edition with silk ribbon marker. Restricted to 7,000 copies.

The Light Fantastic (Isis, 1995). Large print edition (available in both hardback and paperback).

The Light Fantastic (Corgi, 1986). UK paperback edition. 34,100 copies printed.

Discworld 3 – Equal Rites

Equal Rites (Victor Gollancz in association with Colin Smythe, 1987). First UK edition with £9.95 net on inner flap of dustwrapper. Green boards with gilt titles. 2,850 copies printed. Note: Later printings released under Victor Gollancz imprint only.

Equal Rites (Victor Gollancz, 1987). Note: A WH Smith promotional edition is also available.

Equal Rites (Victor Gollancz, 1995). UK compact edition (one of four compact editions released; all four available in a slipcase). 20,000 copies only.

Equal Rites (Isis, 1994). Large print edition in dustwrapper.

Equal Rites (BCA, 2001). Unseen Library edition. Deluxe half-leatherette edition with silk ribbon marker. Restricted to 7,000 copies.

Equal Rites (Corgi, 1987). Paperback edition restricted to 61,000 copies.

Equal Rites released in *The Witches Trilogy* (Victor Gollancz,

1994). Omnibus edition containing *Equal Rites*, *Wyrd Sisters* and *Witches Abroad*. First printing restricted to 10,000 copies exclusively for WH Smith, thereafter on general release.

Discworld 4 – Mort

Mort (Victor Gollancz/Colin Smythe, 1987). UK hardback in priced dustwrapper at £10.95 net. Black cloth boards with gilt titles. 3,950 copies printed.

Mort (Victor Gollancz/Colin Smythe, 1987). Proof copy with dustwrapper. 50–100 copies only.

Mort: The Big Comic illustrated by Graham Higgins (Gollancz, 1994). First UK hardback.

Mort: The Big Comic illustrated by Graham Higgins (Gollancz, 1994). First UK paperback edition.

Mort (Isis, 1995). Large print edition released in hardback and paperback.

Mort (hardback reissue, 1996).

Mort (special promotional edition, WH Smith, 1996).

Mort (BCA, 2002). Unseen Library edition. Deluxe half-leatherette edition with silk ribbon marker. Restricted to 5,000 copies.

Mort (Victor Gollancz, 1998) in *Death Trilogy*. A Discworld omnibus containing *Mort*, *Reaper Man* and *Soul Music*. 22,000 copies. Note: The publicity dustwrapper used the 1974 Josh Kirby painting of the Grim Reaper, which Pratchett didn't approve of.

Mort (Corgi, 1988). UK paperback edition. 111,500 copies. Note: For Christmas 1990 Corgi issued *Mort, Sourcery* and *Wyrd Sisters* in a slipcase.

Mort (WH Smith edition, 2003). 'Little Reads' edition, with opening pages of the novel, 'published in association with Corgi to celebrate the BBC's Big Read'. 30,000 copies.

Mort (new paperback edition, 2004). With black/gold photographic design cover.

Discworld 5 – Sourcery

Sourcery (Victor Gollancz/Colin Smythe, 1988). UK hardback in priced dustwrapper at £10.85. Yellow boards with gilt titles. 7,200 copies.

Sourcery (Victor Gollancz, 1988). Advanced sampler (first 61 pages plus four-page introduction to Discworld).

Sourcery (BCA, 1988). UK book club hardback in dustwrapper.

Sourcery (BCA, 2002). Unseen Library edition. Deluxe half-leatherette edition with silk ribbon marker. Restricted to 5,000 copies.

Sourcery (Victor Gollancz, 2001). Published in *The Rincewind Trilogy*. Omnibus edition containing *Sourcery, Eric* and *Interesting Times*. Hardback. 8,000 copies only.

Sourcery (Corgi, 1989). UK paperback edition.

Discworld 6 – Wyrd Sisters

Wyrd Sisters (Victor Gollancz, 1988). UK hardback in priced dustwrapper at £10.95 net. Green boards and gold titles with white endpapers. 6,700 copies printed.

Wyrd Sisters (Victor Gollancz, 1988). Proof copy. 100 copies printed only.

Wyrd Sisters (BCA, 2002). Unseen Library edition. Deluxe half-leatherette edition with silk ribbon marker. Restricted to 5,000 copies.

Wyrd Sisters (Corgi, 1989). UK paperback edition.

Notes: New issue, with black/gold photographic design cover, on sale at same time as Kirby edition, 2004. For Christmas 1990, Corgi issued *Mort, Sourcery* and *Wyrd Sisters* in a slipcase. In 1994

CRAIG CABELL

Victor Gollancz issued *The Witches Trilogy*, a Discworld omnibus containing *Equal Rites, Wyrd Sisters* and *Witches Abroad*. The first printing of 10,000 copies exclusive to WH Smith for six months; subsequent printings for general sale.

Discworld 7 – Pyramids

Pyramids (Victor Gollancz, 1989). UK hardback in dustwrapper. Black cloth boards with gilt titles. 12,300 copies. Note i: Some copies were issued with a Discworld cup in a display box. Note ii: Review copies of this book were numbered up to at least 249 (the number of the copy inspected for this bibliography) by the publicist and came with a press release.

Pyramids (Victor Gollancz, 1989). Proof copy. 100 copies only.

Pyramids (BCA, 2003). Unseen Library edition. Deluxe half-leatherette edition with silk ribbon marker. Restricted to 4,000 copies.

Omnibus edition (Victor Gollancz, 2000). *The Gods Trilogy* containing *Pyramids, Small Gods* and *Hogfather*. 11,000 copies printed.

Pyramids (Corgi, 1990). First UK paperback edition.

Discworld 8 – Guards! Guards!

Guards! Guards! (Victor Gollancz, 1989). UK hardback in priced dustwrapper at £12.95. Light blue boards with red gilt titles.14,200 copies.

Guards! Guards! (Victor Gollancz, 1989). Proof copy. 100 copies only.

Guards! Guards! (Corgi, 1990). UK paperback edition.

Guards! Guards! illustrated by Graham Higgins (Gollancz, 2000). First UK hardback.

Guards! Guards! illustrated by Graham Higgins (Gollancz,

2000). First UK paperback edition.

Guards! Guards! (BCA, 2003). Unseen Library edition. Deluxe half-leatherette edition with silk ribbon marker. Restricted to 4,000 copies.

Omnibus (Victor Gollancz, 1999). *City Watch Trilogy* containing *Guards! Guards!, Men at Arms* and *Feet of Clay.* 29,800 copies.

Discworld 9 – Eric

Eric (Victor Gollancz, 1990). UK hardback edition in dustwrapper. Black boards with gilt titles. 4,200 copies.

Eric (Victor Gollancz, 1990). UK paperback edition. 50,500 copies.

Eric (Victor Gollancz, 1991). Unillustrated edition. 75,000 copies.

Eric (BCA, 2003). Unseen Library edition. Deluxe half-leatherette edition with silk ribbon marker. Restricted to 4,000 copies.

The Illustrated Eric (Victor Gollancz, 2010). UK hardback with laminated boards.

Omnibus (Victor Gollancz, 2001). *The Rincewind Trilogy*, containing *Sourcery, Eric* and *Interesting Times.* 8,000 copies.

Discworld 10 – Moving Pictures

Moving Pictures (Victor Gollancz, 1990). UK hardback. 18,200 copies.

Moving Pictures (Victor Gollancz, 1990). Proof copy. 100 copies.

Moving Pictures (BCA, 2004). Unseen Library edition. Deluxe half-leatherette edition with silk ribbon marker.

Moving Pictures (Corgi, 1991). UK paperback edition.

Discworld 11 – Reaper Man

Reaper Man (Victor Gollancz, 1991). First UK edition with priced dustwrapper at £13.99 net. Black boards with gold titles. White endpapers. 20,200 copies.

Reaper Man (Victor Gollancz, 1991). Proof copy. 150 copies.

Reaper Man (reissued collector's edition, 1997). 5,400 copies.

Reaper Man (BCA, 2004). Unseen Library edition. Deluxe half-leatherette edition with silk ribbon marker.

Reaper Man (Corgi, 1992). First UK paperback edition.

Omnibus (Victor Gollancz, 1998). *Death Trilogy*, a Discworld omnibus containing *Mort*, *Reaper Man* and *Soul Music*. First printing 22,000 copies. The advance publicity jackets used Josh Kirby's 1974 painting of the Grim Reaper as a colour illustration; the published edition used a detail of *Death in His Study* from *Eric*.

Discworld 12 – Witches Abroad

Witches Abroad (Victor Gollancz, 1991). First UK hardback edition with priced dustwrapper at £13.99 net. Red boards with gold titles. White endpapers. 25,000 copies.

Witches Abroad (Victor Gollancz, 1991). Proof copy. 100 copies only.

Witches Abroad (BCA, 2004). Unseen Library edition. Deluxe half-leatherette edition with silk ribbon marker.

Witches Abroad (Corgi, 1992). UK paperback edition.

Omnibus (Victor Gollancz, 1994). *The Witches Trilogy*, containing *Equal Rites*, *Wyrd Sisters* and *Witches Abroad*. The first printing of 10,000 copies was exclusive to WH Smith for six months; subsequent printings for general sale.

Discworld 13 – Small Gods

Small Gods (Victor Gollancz, 1992). First UK hardback with priced dustwrapper at £14.99. Light brown boards with gilt letting. 27,700 copies.

Small Gods (Victor Gollancz, 1992). Proof copy. 100 copies only.

Small Gods (BCA, 2006). Unseen Library edition. Deluxe half-leatherette edition with silk ribbon marker. Restricted to 3,500 copies.

Omnibus (Victor Gollancz, 2000). *The Gods Trilogy*, containing *Pyramids, Small Gods* and *Hogfather*. 11,000 copies.

Small Gods (Corgi, 1993). UK paperback edition.

Discworld 14 – Lords and Ladies

Lords and Ladies (Victor Gollancz, 1992). First UK hardback in dustwrapper. 30,000 copies.

Lords and Ladies (Victor Gollancz, 1992). Proof copy. 116 copies.

Lords and Ladies (BCA, 2006). Unseen Library edition. Deluxe half-leatherette edition with silk ribbon marker. Restricted to 3,500 copies.

Lords and Ladies (Corgi, 1993). UK paperback edition.

Discworld 15 – Men at Arms

Men at Arms (Victor Gollancz, 1993). First UK edition in priced dustwrapper at £14.99. Red boards with gilt titles. White endpapers. 40,000 copies.

Men at Arms (Victor Gollancz, 1993). Proof copy. 150 copies. Note: Some collectors and general readers enjoy the 'pocket-sized' BCA hardback editions, so it is useful to note that *Men at Arms* was the first to be issued in that format.

Men at Arms (BCA, 2006). Unseen Library edition. Deluxe half-leatherette edition with silk ribbon marker. Restricted to 3,500 copies.

Men at Arms (Corgi, 1994). First UK paperback edition.

Omnibus (Victor Gollancz, 1999). *City Watch Trilogy*, containing *Guards! Guards!*, *Men at Arms* and *Feet of Clay*.

Discworld 16 – Soul Music

Soul Music (Victor Gollancz, 1994). First UK edition in priced dustwrapper at £14.99. 40,000 copies.

Soul Music (Victor Gollancz, 1994). Proof copy. 146 copies.

Soul Music (BCA, 2007). Unseen Library edition. Deluxe half-leatherette edition with silk ribbon marker. 3,000 copies.

Soul Music (Isis, 1997). Large print edition. 550 copies.

Omnibus (Victor Gollancz, 1998). *Death Trilogy*, containing *Mort*, *Reaper Man* and *Soul Music*. First printing 22,000 copies.

Soul Music (Corgi, 1995). First UK paperback edition.

Discworld 17 – Interesting Times

Interesting Times (Victor Gollancz, 1994). First UK hardback in priced dustwrapper. 43,000 copies. Blue boards.

Interesting Times (Victor Gollancz, 1994). Proof copy. 250 copies.

Interesting Times (BCA, 2007). Unseen Library edition. Deluxe half-leatherette edition with silk ribbon marker. Restricted to 3,000 copies.

Interesting Times (Isis, 1995). Large print edition, issued in both hardback and paperback.

Interesting Times (Corgi, 1995). First UK paperback edition.

Omnibus (Victor Gollancz, 2001). *The Rincewind Trilogy*,

containing *Sourcery, Eric* and *Interesting Times*. First printing 8,000 copies.

Discworld 18 – Maskerade

Maskerade (Victor Gollancz, 1995). First UK hardback in priced dustwrapper. 55,000 copies. Burgundy boards.

Maskerade (Victor Gollancz, 1995). Proof copy. 189 copies.

Maskerade (Corgi, 1996). First UK paperback edition.

Maskerade (Isis, 1996). Large print edition. 500 copies.

Maskerade (BCA, 2007). Unseen Library edition. Deluxe half-leatherette edition with silk ribbon marker. Restricted to 3,000 copies. Note: Copies were initially sent out with the title *Maskarade*, but these were withdrawn and replaced by copies with the correct title. Any original copies that still exist are worth considerably more.

Discworld 19 – Feet of Clay

Feet of Clay (Victor Gollancz, 1996). First UK edition in priced dustwrapper at £15.99. Grey boards with gilt titles. White endpapers. 85,000 copies.

Feet of Clay (Victor Gollancz, 1996). Proof copy. 167 copies.

Feet of Clay (Corgi, 1997). First UK paperback edition.

Omnibus (Victor Gollancz, 1999). *The City Watch Trilogy*, containing *Guards! Guards!, Men at Arms* and *Feet of Clay*. 29,800 copies.

Discworld 20 – Hogfather

Hogfather (Victor Gollancz, 1996). First UK hardback in priced dustwrapper at £15.99. Blue boards with gilt titles. 70,000 copies.

Hogfather (Victor Gollancz, 1996). Proof copy. 196 copies.

Hogfather (Corgi, 1997). First UK paperback edition.

Omnibus (Victor Gollancz, 2000). *The Gods Trilogy*, containing *Pyramids, Small Gods* and *Hogfather.* 11,000 copies.

Hogfather (Corgi, 2006). Sky One paperback tie-in edition.

Discworld 21 – Jingo

Jingo (Victor Gollancz, 1997). First UK hardback in priced dustwrapper at £16.99. Black boards with gilt titles.120,000 copies.

Jingo (Victor Gollancz, 1997). Proof copy. 170 copies.

Jingo (Corgi, 1998). First UK paperback edition.

Discworld 22 – The Last Continent

The Last Continent (Doubleday, 1998). First UK edition in priced dustwrapper at £16.99. Red boards with gilt titles. 93,500 copies. Note: Two versions of the first printing exist. An initial quantity for Australia of 10,000 copies had deep blue endpapers and plain spine blocking, while those for the home market had red endpapers and spine blocking that used the same lettering as the dustwrapper.

The Last Continent (Doubleday, 1998). Proof copy. 100 copies only.

The Last Continent (Corgi, 1999). First UK paperback edition.

The Last Continent (Charnwood/Thorpe/Ulverscroft, 2005). Large print hardback edition.

Discworld 23 – Carpe Jugulum

Carpe Jugulum (Doubleday, 1998). First UK edition in priced dustwrapper at £16.99. Black boards with gilt titles. Red endpapers. 160,000 copies.

Carpe Jugulum (Doubleday, 1998). Proof copy. 148 copies.

Carpe Jugulum (Charnwood/Thorpe/Ulverscroft, 2005). Large print hardback in dustwrapper.

Carpe Jugulum (Corgi, 1999). First UK paperback edition. Note: 40,000 copies printed for the New World market (Australia and New Zealand); 322,000 copies for the British market with the cover illustration reproduced on a smaller scale (both listed as first printing). An easy way to tell the difference is to look for a shoe jutting into the title box on the front cover of the New World copy; the British counterpart doesn't have this detail.

Discworld 24 – The Fifth Elephant

The Fifth Elephant (Doubleday, 1999). First UK hardback in priced dustwrapper at £16.99. Red boards with gilt titles.

The Fifth Elephant (Doubleday, 1999). Proof copy. 155 copies.

The Fifth Elephant (Corgi, 2000). First UK paperback edition.

The Fifth Elephant (Charnwood/Thorpe/Ulverscroft, 2000). Large print edition. 550 copies.

Discworld 25 – The Truth

The Truth (Doubleday, 2000). First UK edition in priced dustwrapper at £16.99. Blue boards with gilt titles with Discworld titled endpapers.

The Truth (Doubleday, 2000). Proof copy. 370 copies. Note: Of these, 200 copies were signed by Pratchett for special presentation purposes to mark the 25th anniversary of Discworld. Unsigned copies are consequently more limited and worth more in pristine condition.

CRAIG CABELL

The Truth (Corgi, 2001). First UK paperback edition.

The Truth (Charnwood/Thorpe, 2003). Large print hardback edition.

Discworld 26 – Thief of Time

Thief of Time (Doubleday, 2001). First UK edition in priced dustwrapper at £16.99. Black boards with gilt titles. Orange endpapers. Full number string to copyright page.

Thief of Time (Doubleday, 2001). Proof copy. 100 copies only with title error – *The Thief of Time* – on cover.

Thief of Time (Corgi, 2002). First UK paperback edition. Note: Some advanced copies were distributed with publicity material.

Thief of Time (Charnwood/ Thorpe/Ulverscroft, 2002). Large print hardback in dustwrapper. 550 copies.

Discworld 27 – The Last Hero

The Last Hero (Victor Gollancz, 2001). First edition in priced dustwrapper at £17.99. 175,000 copies.

The Last Hero (Victor Gollancz, 2001). Proof copy. Colour 16-page sampler.

The Last Hero (Victor Gollancz, 2001). Deluxe edition in slipcase. Limited to 2,000 copies.

The Last Hero (Victor Gollancz, 2002). Second edition with eight new illustrations and 'scream' cover.

The Last Hero (Victor Gollancz, 2002). First UK paperback edition.

The Last Hero (Victor Gollancz, 2007). Mass market paperback edition.

Discworld 28 – The Amazing Maurice and his Educated Rodents

The Amazing Maurice and his Educated Rodents (Doubleday, 2001). First UK hardback in priced dustwrapper at £12.99. Dark blue boards with gilt titles. Yellow endpapers.

The Amazing Maurice and his Educated Rodents (Doubleday, 2001). Proof copy. 430 copies.

The Amazing Maurice and his Educated Rodents (Isis, 2001). Large print edition in dustwrapper.

The Amazing Maurice and his Educated Rodents (Corgi, 2002). First UK paperback edition.

The Amazing Maurice and his Educated Rodents (Heinemann/New Windmills series, 2004). Educational edition.

Discworld 29 – Night Watch

Night Watch (Doubleday, 2002). First UK edition in priced dustwrapper at £17.99. Black boards with gilt titles. Red endpapers. Full number line to copyright page.

Night Watch (Doubleday, 2002). First UK edition in priced dustwrapper at £17.99. Black boards with gilt titles. Red endpapers. Full number line to copyright page. With letter from publisher stating that it is one of only nine copies flat signed and sent as a runner-up prize in a Terry Pratchett competition.

Night Watch (Corgi, 2003). First UK paperback edition.

Night Watch (Thorpe/Charnwood, 2004). Large print edition in dustwrapper.

Discworld 30 – The Wee Free Men

The Wee Free Men (Doubleday, 2003). First UK edition in priced dustwrapper at £12.99. Deep purple boards with gilt titles. Yellow endpapers. Full number string to copyright page.

The Wee Free Men (Doubleday, 2003). Poof copy. 200 copies.

The Wee Free Men (Corgi, 2004). First UK paperback edition.

The Wee Free Men (Isis, 2010). Large print edition in hardback and paperback.

The Illustrated Wee Free Men (Doubleday, 2008). First UK hardback edition in priced dustwrapper at £14.99. Illustrated by Stephen Player.

Discworld 31 – Monstrous Regiment

Monstrous Regiment (Doubleday, 2003). First UK edition in priced dustwrapper at £17.99. Black boards with gilt titles. Red endpapers with full number string to copyright page. Note: Copies printed in Australia lack the price on the inside front flap of the dustwrapper.

Monstrous Regiment (Corgi, 2004). First UK paperback edition.

Monstrous Regiment (Charnwood/Thorpe, 2003). First UK large print edition.

Discworld 32 – A Hat Full of Sky

A Hat Full of Sky (Doubleday, 2004). First UK edition in priced dustwrapper at £12.99. Deep purple boards with gilt titles. Scorched orange endpapers. Full number string to copyright page.

A Hat Full of Sky (Doubleday, 2004). UK uncorrected proof in green illustrated card cover. 490 copies.

A Hat Full of Sky (Corgi, 2005). First UK paperback edition.

Discworld 33 - Going Postal

Going Postal (Doubleday, 2004). First UK edition in priced dustwrapper at £17.99. Black boards with gilt titles. Coloured postage stamps endpapers. Full number string on copyright page.

Going Postal (Doubleday, 2004). Proof copy. 727 copies.

Going Postal (Doubleday, 2004). Galley proof, parcel wrapped in string with address card.

Going Postal (Thorpe/Charnwood, 2004). Large print edition.

Discworld 34 - Thud!

Thud! (Doubleday, 2005). First UK edition. Priced dustwrapper at £17.99. Black boards with gilt titles. White patterned endpapers with full number string to copyright page.

Thud! (Doubleday, 2005). First UK edition. Ten copies flat signed by Pratchett for competition prize, sent to winners with a letter of congratulations from the publisher.

Thud! (Doubleday, 2005). Proof copy. 108 copies.

Thud! (Doubleday, 2005). Limited slipcase edition of 1,000 copies.

Thud! (Charnwood/Thorpe, 2006). Large print hardback in dustwrapper.

Discworld 35 - Wintersmith

Wintersmith (Doubleday, 2006). First UK edition in priced dustwrapper at £14.99. Blue boards with gilt titles. Full number string to copyright page.

Wintersmith (Doubleday, 2006). Proof copy. 120 copies.

Wintersmith (Doubleday, 2006). Signed and numbered collector's edition. 1,000 copies.

Wintersmith (Doubleday, 2006). First UK trade paperback

edition (released simultaneously with first edition hardback).

Wintersmith (Corgi, 2007). First UK paperback edition.

Wintersmith (Corgi, 2007). Black and gold UK paperback edition.

Discworld 36 – Making Money

Making Money (Doubleday, 2007). First UK edition in priced dustwrapper at £18.99. Black boards with gilt titles. Full number string to copyright page.

Making Money (Doubleday, 2007). Proof copy. 150 copies.

Making Money (Doubleday, 2007). Specially bound and numbered. 2,500 signed copies in slipcase. Cheque book and bank notes were also issued as publicity material for Waterstone's and Borders.

Making Money (Corgi, 2008). First UK paperback edition.

Making Money (Doubleday, 2007). Free sampler featuring an extract from Chapter One, released to celebrate the 25th anniversary of Discworld. Also released was a 'Free Waterstone's exclusive introduction to Terry Pratchett's Discworld' containing the same extract, and an 'Introduction to Discworld' by Michael Rowley, Waterstone's buyer of science fiction and fantasy.

Making Money (BCA, 2007). UK hardback in dustwrapper.

Making Money (Thorpe/Charnwood, 2008). Large print edition. Hardback in dustwrapper.

Discworld 37 – Unseen Academicals

Unseen Academicals (Doubleday, 2009). First UK edition in priced dustwrapper at £18.99. Brown boards with gilt titles. Orange endpapers. Full number line to copyright page. Note: Waterstone's exclusive copy has sticker on cover with an unopened packet of collector's cards mounted on inside back board.

Unseen Academicals (Doubleday, 2007). Proof copy (some copies signed and stamped). 145 copies.

Unseen Academicals (Doubleday, 2009). First UK edition. In addition to the standard trade edition, 3,000 numbered, specially bound and slipcased copies were produced as a 'limited collector's edition' for Waterstone's. These did not have a separate ISBN.

Unseen Academicals (Corgi, 2010). First paperback edition.

Unseen Academicals (Thorpe/Charnwood, 2010). First large print UK edition.

Discworld 38 – I Shall Wear Midnight

I Shall Wear Midnight (Doubleday, 2010). First UK edition in priced dustwrapper at £18.99. Black boards with gilt titles. Dark blue endpapers. Full number line to copyright page. Note: Waterstone's exclusive copy came with sticker on cover with an unopened packet attached to rear inner board with a Discworld colour print.

I Shall Wear Midnight (Doubleday, 2010). Trade paperback edition.

I Shall Wear Midnight (Doubleday, 2010). Proof copy. 153 copies, some signed and stamped.

I Shall Wear Midnight (Isis, 2010). Large print edition hardback.

I Shall Wear Midnight (Isis, 2010). Large print edition paperback.

I Shall Wear Midnight (Doubleday, 2010). Collectors' edition, with additional treatise by Jacqueline Simpson on the folklore in the book, an extra illustration by Paul Kidby, special binding, in slipcase. Exclusive to Amazon and limited to 2,500 copies.

I Shall Wear Midnight (Doubleday, 2010). 350 copies sold and signed at midnight at Waterstone's Piccadilly, with 'free limited edition print' at end of book, title page signed by Terry Pratchett and stamped 'signed at midnight' and 'official signature'. Some copies are also signed by the artist as well.

I Shall Wear Midnight (Doubleday, 2010). 'Special fans' cover. Released November 2010. Approximately 3,000 copies issued with dustwrapper with the jacket design printed over a mosaic of Facebook portraits of 2,000 'special fans'. The jacket alone has a different ISBN (978-0-857-53056-1).

Discworld 39 – Snuff

Snuff (Doubleday, 2011). First UK hardback in priced dustwrapper.

Snuff (Corgi, 2012). First UK paperback edition.

THE JOHNNY MAXWELL SERIES

Only You Can Save Mankind (Doubleday, 1992). First UK hardback in priced dustwrapper at £9.99. Black boards with gilt titles. White endpapers. 16,700 copies.

Only You Can Save Mankind (Corgi, 1993). First UK paperback edition.

Only You Can Save Mankind (Galaxy/Chivers, 1996). Large print hardback edition.

Only You Can Save Mankind (Doubleday, 2004). UK special limited edition. 1,000 numbered copies printed for the world premiere of the musical *Only You Can Save Mankind* at the Edinburgh Fringe Festival, 2004.

Johnny and the Dead (Doubleday, 1993). First UK edition in priced dustwrapper at £9.99. Grey boards and gold titles. White endpapers. 22,400 copies.

Johnny and the Dead (Doubleday, 1993). Limited edition. Ten copies bound in quarter dark blue leatherette with cloth boards and signed by Terry Pratchett for a competition run by Books Etc.

Johnny and the Dead (Corgi, 1994). First UK paperback edition. 122,500 copies.

Johnny and the Dead (Galaxy/Chivers, 1997). Large print hardback in dustwrapper.

Johnny and the Bomb (Doubleday, 1996). First UK edition in priced dustwrapper at £12.99. Mustard boards and gold titles. White endpapers. 24,900 copies.

Johnny and the Bomb (Corgi, 1997). First UK paperback edition. 105,000 copies.

The Johnny Maxwell Trilogy (Doubleday, 1999). Contains *Only You Can Save Mankind, Johnny and the Dead* and *Johnny and the Bomb*. First UK edition in priced dustwrapper. Black boards.

The Johnny Maxwell Collection (Corgi, 2005). Slipcase paperback edition, containing *Only You Can Save Mankind, Johnny and the Dead* and *Johnny and the Bomb*.

NATION

Nation (Doubleday Young Books, 2008). First UK hardback in priced dustwrapper at £16.99. Deep purple boards with gilt titles. Night blue illustrated endpapers. Full number line to copyright page.

Nation (Doubleday Young Books, 2008). Proof copy. 120 copies.

Nation (Doubleday Young Books, 2008). Limited edition of 275 copies, numbered and signed by the author. Note: Several unnumbered and consequently unsigned copies have also been seen by the author while compiling this bibliography.

Nation (Doubleday Young Books, 2008). Waterstone's black

cover edition. Limited to 5,000 copies. Note: A black cover paperback edition was also released for Father's Day.

Nation (Doubleday Young Books, 2008). Trade paperback edition.

Nation (Corgi, 2009). First UK paperback edition.

Nation (Isis, 2009). Large print hardback and paperback editions.

MISCELLANEOUS

The Unadulterated Cat (Victor Gollancz, 1989). Part proof copy with proof wrapper. Approximately 200 copies.

The Unadulterated Cat (Victor Gollancz, 1989). Large format paperback edition. 50,250 copies.

The Unadulterated Cat (Victor Gollancz, 1992). Standard paperback edition.

The Unadulterated Cat (Victor Gollancz, 2002). Reissue. First UK hardback edition, with additional illustrations.

'The Secret Book of the Dead'. Poem. First published in *Now We Are Sick: An Anthology of Nasty Verse*, edited by Neil Gaiman and Stephen Jones (Dreamhaven Books, Minneapolis, MN, 1991). Limited signed edition. 300 copies in lexohyde bonded leather were signed by the contributors: 250 numbered, for sale; 50 lettered and given to the contributors. 1000 unsigned copies bound in Skivertex.

Good Omens (with Neil Gaiman) (Victor Gollancz, 1990). First UK edition in priced dustwrapper.

Good Omens (Victor Gollancz, 1990). Proof copy. Print run unknown.

Good Omens (Victor Gollancz, 1990). 46-page sampler. Print run unknown but deemed to be more common than full proof.

Good Omens (Corgi, 1991). First UK paperback edition. Note: The first printing had Pratchett's name first on the cover and Gaiman's second, but the reverse order on the title page. The title page was corrected in subsequent printings.

Good Omens (Fantasy & SF Book Club, 2003). Complete with new introduction from the authors. Part of the 25th Birthday Library Collection.

Good Omens (Victor Gollancz, 2007). New hardback edition with white front and black back to cover.

Truckers (Doubleday, 1989). First UK edition in dustwrapper.

Truckers adapted by Brian Trueman (Corgi, 1992).

Truckers simplified (Ladybird, 1992). Small hardback with laminated boards.

Diggers (Doubleday, 1990). First UK edition in dustwrapper.

Diggers (Doubleday, 1990). Proof copy.

Wings (Doubleday, 1990). First UK edition in dustwrapper..

Note: *Truckers*, *Diggers* and *Wings* come under the collective title *The Bromeliad Trilogy*.

*Once More ** with Footnotes* (NEFS, 2004). Special edition hardback featuring early and rare Pratchett material. Some copies exist signed. Primarily a US release.

Where's My Cow? (Doubleday, 2005). UK hardback edition.

Ankh-Morpork City Watch Warrant Card (2005). 10,000 copies written by Pratchett for Waterstone's by the Cunning Artificer.

The First 3 Discworld Volumes (Corgi, 1989). Three UK paperbacks in slipcase (*The Colour of Magic*, *The Light Fantastic* and *Equal Rites*). Special Christmas edition.

The Next 3 Discworld Volumes (Corgi, 1990). Three UK paperbacks in slipcase (*Mort, Sourcery* and *Wyrd Sisters*). Special Christmas edition.

Discworld Starter Pack (Corgi, 1991). *The Colour of Magic, The Light Fantastic* and *Equal Rites*, issued for Ottakars. A signed, slipcase copy of *The Colour of Magic* together with a 'Discworld Starter Pack'; a slipcase containing paperbacks of the first three Discworld novels.

The Witches Trilogy (Victor Gollancz, 1994). A Discworld omnibus including *Equal Rites, Wyrd Sisters* and *Witches Abroad*. 21, 250 copies. 10,000 copies contained a note that they had been produced exclusively for WH Smith.

The Compact Edition (Victor Gollancz, 1995). Small illustrated boards in a slipcase. Includes *The Colour of Magic, The Light Fantastic, Equal Rites* and *Mort*. 20,000 copies.

The Josh Kirby Poster Book, Inspired by Terry Pratchett's Discworld Novels (Corgi, 1990).

The Josh Kirby Discworld Portfolio (Dragon's World, 1993).

The Streets of Ankh-Morpork (Corgi, 1993).

The First Discworld Novels (Colin Smythe, 1999). First UK hardback in priced dustwrapper. Includes *The Colour of Magic* and *The Light Fantastic*.

Terry Pratchett with Stephen Briggs, *The Discworld Companion* (Victor Gollancz, 1994). First UK edition in priced dustwrapper. 32,750 copies.

Terry Pratchett with Stephen Briggs, *The Discworld Companion* (Victor Gollancz, 1994). Proof copy. 64-page sampler. 392 copies.

Terry Pratchett with Stephen Briggs, *The Discworld Companion* (Victor Gollancz, 1995). First UK paperback edition. 70,000 copies.

The Pratchett Portfolio (Victor Gollancz, 1996). Compendium of characters from the Discworld. Illustrated by Paul Kidby. UK paperback edition. 25,000 copies.

The Pratchett Portfolio (Victor Gollancz, 1996). Proof copy. Eight-page sampler. 300 copies.

'Twenty Pence with envelope and seasonal Greeting'. Short story. (*Time Out* magazine, 16–30 December 1987). Christmas issue.

'Twenty Pence with envelope and seasonal Greeting'. Short story. Reprinted in *Shivers for Christmas* (Michael O'Mara Books, 1995).

'Twenty Pence with envelope and seasonal Greeting'. Short story. Reprinted in *Shivers for Christmas* (Ulverscroft Foundation, 1996). Large print edition.

'Twenty Pence with envelope and seasonal Greeting'. Short story. Reprinted in *Shivers for Christmas*. Reprinted with introductory note in *Once More★ ★with footnotes*, eds Sheila Perry and Priscilla Olson (NEFSA Press, 2004).

Terry Pratchett and Stephen Briggs, *Discworld's Unseen University Diary* (Victor Gollancz, 1997). 30,000 copies.

Terry Pratchett and Stephen Briggs, *Discworld's Ankh-Morpork City Watch Diary 1999* (Victor Gollancz, 1998). 35,000 copies.

Terry Pratchett and Stephen Briggs, *Discworld Assassin's Guild Yearbook and Diary 2000* (Victor Gollancz, 1999).

Terry Pratchett and Stephen Briggs, *Discworld Fools' Guild Yearbook and Diary 2001* (Victor Gollancz, 2000). Note: Extracts published in *The Joey*, the official magazine of Clowns International, Issue 69, March 2005.

Terry Pratchett and Stephen Briggs, *Discworld Thieves' Guild Yearbook and Diary 2002* (Victor Gollancz, 2001).

Terry Pratchett and Stephen Briggs, *Discworld (Reformed) Vampyre's Diary 2003* (Victor Gollancz, 2002).

CRAIG CABELL

Terry Pratchett with Stephen Briggs, *Ankh-Morpork Post Office Handbook and Discworld Diary 2007* (Victor Gollancz, 2006).

Terry Pratchett's Discworld Collector's Edition 1999 Calendar (The Ink Group, 1998).

Terry Pratchett's Discworld Collector's Edition 1999 Day-to-day Calendar (The Ink Group, 1998).

Terry Pratchett's Discworld Collector's Edition 2000 Day-to-day Calendar (The Ink Group, 1999).

Terry Pratchett's 2000 Discworld Collector's Edition Calendar (The Ink Group, 1999). Wall calendar.

Terry Pratchett's 2001 Discworld Collector's Edition Calendar (The Ink Group, 2000). Wall calendar.

Terry Pratchett's Discworld Collector's Edition 2002 Calendar (Victor Gollancz, 2001). Wall calendar.

Terry Pratchett's Discworld Collector's Edition 2003 Calendar (Victor Gollancz, 2002). Wall calendar.

Terry Pratchett's Discworld Collector's Edition 2004 Calendar (Victor Gollancz, 2003). Wall calendar.

Terry Pratchett's Discworld Collector's Edition 2005 Calendar (Victor Gollancz, 2004). Wall calendar.

Terry Pratchett's Discworld Collector's Edition 2006 Calendar (Victor Gollancz, 2005). Wall calendar.

Terry Pratchett's Hogfather Discworld Calendar 2007 (Victor Gollancz, 2006). Wall calendar.

Terry Pratchett's Discworld Collector's Edition 2008 Calendar (Victor Gollancz, 2007). Wall calendar.

Terry Pratchett's Discworld Collector's Edition 2009 Calendar (Victor Gollancz, 2008). Wall calendar.

Terry Pratchett's Discworld Collector's Edition 2010 Calendar (Victor Gollancz, 2009). Wall calendar.

Terry Pratchett's Discworld Collector's Edition 2011 Calendar – wall calendar (Victor Gollancz, 2010). Wall calendar.

Terry Pratchett's Discworld Collector's Edition 2012 Calendar (Victor Gollancz, 2011). Wall calendar.

Terry Pratchett and Stephen Briggs, *Nanny Ogg's Cook Book* (Doubleday, 1999). First UK hardback edition.
Terry Pratchett and Stephen Briggs, *Nanny Ogg's Cook Book* (Corgi, 2001). First UK paperback edition.
Terry Pratchett and Paul Kidby, *Death's Domain* (Corgi, 1999). 34,100 copies.

Terry Pratchett, Ian Stewart and Jack Cohen, *The Science of Discworld* (Ebury Press, 1999). UK hardback edition. 20,022 copies.
Terry Pratchett, Ian Stewart and Jack Cohen, *The Science of Discworld* (Ebury Press, 1999). Proof copy. 500 copies.
Terry Pratchett, Ian Stewart and Jack Cohen, *The Science of Discworld II: The Globe* (Ebury Press, 2002). UK hardback edition. 33,500 copies.
Terry Pratchett, Ian Stewart and Jack Cohen, *The Science of Discworld II: The Globe* (Ebury Press, 2002). Proof copy. 500 copies.
Terry Pratchett, Ian Stewart and Jack Cohen, *The Science of Discworld II: The Globe* (Ebury Press, 2003). First UK paperback edition.
Terry Pratchett, Ian Stewart and Jack Cohen, *The Science of Discworld III: Darwin's Watch* (Ebury Press, 2005). First UK hardback edition.

Discworld Almanac (Corgi, 2004). First UK hardback edition.

Paul Kidby and Terry Pratchett, *The Art of Discworld* (Victor Gollancz, 2004). First UK hardback edition.
Terry Pratchett and Jacqueline Simpson, *The Folklore of Discworld*

(Doubleday, 2008). First UK hardback edition in priced dustwrapper at £17.99. Black boards with gilt titles. Tan endpapers.

Terry Pratchett and Jacqueline Simpson, *The Folklore of Discworld* (Corgi, 2009). First UK paperback edition. Noted second edition with additional material on *Unseen Academicals*.

SCREENPLAYS

Soul Music: The illustrated screenplay (Corgi, 1997). 10,000 copies.

Wyrd Sisters: The illustrated screenplay (Corgi, 1997). 10,000 copies.

Hogfather: The illustrated screenplay (Victor Gollancz, 2006). First UK hardback edition.

Hogfather: The illustrated screenplay (Victor Gollancz, 2009). First UK paperback edition.

The Colour of Magic: The illustrated screenplay (Victor Gollancz, 2008). First UK hardback edition.

GRAPHIC NOVELS

Terry Pratchett's The Colour of Magic: The Graphic Novel. Illustrated by Steven Ross. Adapted by Scott Rockwell. Lettered by Vickie Williams. Edited by David Campiti. Cover illustration by Daerick Gross, Sr. Originally published as a four-issue comic by Innovation in 1991. First paperback edition published by Corgi in 1992.

Terry Pratchett's The Light Fantastic: The Graphic Novel. Illustrated by Steven Ross and Joe Bennet. Adapted by Scott Rockwell. Lettered by Michelle Beck and Vickie Williams. Edited by David Campiti. Cover illustration by Steven Ross. Originally published as a four-issue comic by Innovative Corporation in 1992. First Corgi complete paperback edition 1993.

Mort: A Discworld Big Comic. Illustrated by Graham Higgins (VG Graphics, 1994). First UK hardback edition.

Mort: A Discworld Big Comic. Illustrated by Graham Higgins (VG Graphics, 1994). Proof copy. 16-page sampler. 320 copies.

Mort: A Discworld Big Comic. Illustrated by Graham Higgins (VG Graphics, 1994). First UK paperback edition.

SPECIAL INTRODUCTIONS

Introduction to Roy Lewis, *The Evolution Man* (Corgi, 1989).

Introduction to *The Josh Kirby Poster Book, As Inspired By Terry Pratchett's Discworld Novels* (Corgi, 1989). 25,500 copies.

'About the Author' in *The Arts of Falconrie and Hawking: A Begginners Guide*, by Hodgesaargh! (David Hodges) and Terry Pratchett. 'Published by the Great Dyskworld Publishing Company, 1998, Treacle Mine Road, Ankh-Morpork.' (A footnote on the title page states: 'Terry Pratchett wrote "About the Author".'.) This work has been described as a monument to the Ankh-Morpork publishing industry's traditional hate relationship with dictionaries. 500 copies, with 500 reprinted in 1999.

Foreword to *The Ultimate Encyclopedia of Fantasy. The Definitive Illustrated Guide*, general editor David Pringle (Carlton Books, 1998).

'An Appreciation of Sharpe' in *Sharpe's Trafalgar* by Bernard Cornwell (Scorpion Press, 1999). Limited edition, bound in quarter artificial leather and marbled paper-covered boards. 99 numbered copies signed by the author. 15 lettered deluxe copies bound in quarter real goatskin with raised bands on spine, signed by the author and Terry Pratchett, were produced for private distribution.

Foreword to *Brewer's Dictionary of Phrase & Fable*, Millennium edition, revised by Adrian Room (Cassell, 1999).

Introduction to David Langford's *The Leaky Establishment* (Big Engine, 2001).

Foreword to Jane Dorner's *Creative Web Writing* (A&C Black, 2002).

Foreword to *Brewer's Dictionary of Phrase & Fable*, seventeenth edition, revised by John Ayto (Weidenfeld & Nicolson, 2005). Different from the foreword written for the Millennium edition.

Foreword to *Writers' & Artists' Yearbook 2006* (A&C Black, 2005).

'Everything Under One Roof' in *The Unseen University Cut-out Book* by Terry Pratchett, Alan Batley & Bernard Pearson (Doubleday, 2006). Although the book is stated to have been co-authored, Pratchett's contribution was restricted to writing the introduction.

'A Slightly Worn But Still Quite Lovely Foreword' in *Prince of Stories: The Many Worlds of Neil Gaiman* by Hank Wagner, Christopher Golden and Stephen R Bissette (St Martin's Press, New York, 2008). This originally appeared under the title 'Terry Pratchett on Neil Gaiman' in the 2006 William Morrow edition of *Good Omens*.

Foreword to *Salisbury in Detail* (Salisbury Civic Society, 2009).

Foreword to *Out of the Shadows, Blinking in the Light. My name is not dementia: people with dementia discuss quality of life indicators* (Alzheimer's Society, 2010).

Foreword to *Elves: Nasty or Nice? A Treatise* by Jaqueline[sic] Simpson. (The Discworld Emporium, 2010). Limited edition of 500.

Christmas greeting card showing a greedy king (Colin Smythe Limited). Copies also printed for The National Listening Library (1976).

Discworld picture cards: football collection (2011).

Note on bibliography: Where there are detailed descriptions of rare books, including cloth, priced wrappers, etc, a copy of the book was inspected while compiling this bibliography. In other cases the basic facts are given. A large segment of the bibliography was compiled from the author's own collection.

'Crivens!'

The Unseen Library Bibliography

Restricted access. Wizards of either sex may apply for library ticket from Ook.

CONCLUSION

And Finally

'It is important that we know where we come from,
because if you do not know where you come from, then
you don't know where you are, and if you don't know
where you are, then you don't know where you're
going. And if you don't know where you're going,
you're probably going wrong.'
(Author's Note, *I Shall Wear Midnight*)

Terry Pratchett's fantasy novels are full of life, colour and whimsy. They emanate the personality of the man himself. What is very nice is the fact that if one reads Pratchett's novels in order of publication (from his earliest short stories in the *Bucks Free Press* through to his latest novels), one can witness his growing credentials as a great writer of fantasy.

Pratchett has always been very honest about his relationship with the fantasy genre. It is clear that he broke it down just to rebuild and release it to a new generation of readers and would-be writers who claim the man as a major influence.

233

It is true that his later Discworld novels have a darker side to them – more so than the earlier ones – but whether this is through his illness or a desire to make more of a social comment is for the individual to decide. (Personally, I think it's a bit of both.) I don't think the novels have suffered as a consequence. Perhaps they have become slightly more 'adult', but younger readers have so much to enjoy in other series before progressing to Discworld. Indeed, where would any school library be without *Johnny and the Bomb* and *The Carpet People*?

Like any great artist, Pratchett has fans who favour different periods of his work. I, like others, prefer the earlier Discworld novels, where the characters have no fixed abode and 'anything goes' seems to be the watchword. It is only in those books that the imagination flows thick and fast, in streaming technicolour. *The Colour of Magic*, *The Light Fantastic*, *Equal Rites* and *Mort* are timeless classics that will entertain and influence generations to come. Personally, I also love the Nac Mac Feegle, but after *The Wee Free Men* they never seemed to be in a novel long enough for my liking. Is that a criticism? No, just an observation. The witches and wizards are the people in Pratchett's novels and Pratchett loves people – that's why they are the main characters. The Grim Reaper may hang like the sword of Damocles above the series' head, but perhaps that's now a perfect metaphor for Pratchett's own life, where he faces – so positively – his own demon of a disease. The work Pratchett has done for Alzheimer's sufferers will prove to be as important as his books in years to come, and we will look back in awe at an incredibly imaginative, good, kind and intelligent man, who made a real difference during his life. He is not only the spirit of fantasy, he is the spirit of man personified. That is a big compliment, but a fully justified one.

At the head of this conclusion I included a quote from Pratchett about the individual and their place in the world. I couldn't agree more with this comment. Some people research their family history to find that they weren't from London as the past three generations of their family were led to believe. Instead, the family went back a thousand years as farmers in the West Country and then back to ancient Rome, or something else equally fantastic. This connection with the identity of one's ancestors is important, but so is the identity of who you are today and your place within your immediate family and friends and colleagues. Pratchett's pragmatism with regard to his life today and how he can make a difference to the lives of people around him – interested in him, sharing the same illness as him – is important to the way we should conduct ourselves in everyday life, with dignity and grace.

Terry Pratchett has proved to be a worthy hero to many people and he and his works will continue to thrill and delight his legions of fans for many years to come. The Johnny Maxwell series is an incredibly important one. Basically for children, the books say a lot about the preservation of your local town. When Johnny wakes up in the morning, the whole universe hits him in the face and I'm absolutely convinced that his extra perception is a direct parallel with Pratchett himself. If you really want to see the spirit of fantasy as a youngster, then read *Only You Can Save Mankind*, *Johnny and the Dead* and *Johnny and the Bomb*, because Johnny Maxwell is, to me, Sir Terry Pratchett as a youngster. I only wish he would write a fourth book in the series to show us what Johnny did when he grew up… but perhaps we know that already.

'Rough winds do shake the darling buds of May,
And summer's lease hath all too short a date.'

William Shakespeare (Sonnet 18)

End Note

The frustrating thing with writing this book was having to leave out huge chunks of the Pratchett universe. A whole book could be written about the Night Watch and the Discworld crime novel alone, but it wasn't relevant to the subject matter of the book.

I've written several books now about a writer and his works, but this was the first about a writer and his *key* works. In that respect it became a very self-indulgent book, as I read what was in my opinion the very best Pratchett books relevant to this idea.

The one thing I've learned by writing books about people such as James Herbert and Ian Rankin is that authors give so much more of themselves in their early works, so I make no apology for focusing largely on Pratchett's early novels. Other key works – and series – have been showcased, but it is the early ones that are the most telling and therefore get the most attention when it comes to the conception of the Discworld series and how Pratchett created his artistic direction. The exception to that is *Nation*, a one-off book that was wildly different from any other created by Pratchett and that perhaps addressed where he was as a writer nearly 40 years after breathing life into *The Carpet People*.

Clearly there is much to discuss regarding Pratchett and his life and works. Some of the chapters have been light and fun to write, while others dealt with issues closer to the heart and therefore took a contrasting, more serious swerve. Perhaps these latter chapters were ultimately the more satisfying to write, as they were filled with burning issues that aren't faced just by Terry Pratchett but also by many people from many walks of life, and ultimately that's what the whole Discworld series has done: it has affected people – for the better – from many walks of life.

Craig Cabell
London, June 2011

Further Reading

The following books are considered some of the greatest fantasy novels published. They do not include novels from either the science fiction or horror genres. It is not an exhaustive list but these books certainly allowed me to form an explanation of what the fantasy genre meant to me.

The works of Terry Pratchett, most notably: *The Colour of Magic, The Light Fantastic, Equal Rites, Mort, Sourcery, Pyramids, Eric, Reaper Man, The Wee Free Men, A Hat Full of Sky, Guards! Guards!, Small Gods, Johnny and the Dead, Johnny and the Bomb, Going Postal, Making Money, Nation, I Shall Wear Midnight*.
The fairy books of Andrew Lang: *Blue Fairy Book* (1889), *Red Fairy Book* (1890), *Green Fairy Book* (1892), *Yellow Fairy Book* (1894), *Pink Fairy Book* (1897), *Grey Fairy Book* (1900), *Violet Fairy Book* (1901), *Crimson Fairy Book* (1903), *Brown Fairy Book* (1904), *Orange Fairy Book* (1906), *Olive Fairy Book* (1907), *Lilac Fairy Book* (1910).

A Midsummer Night's Dream, William Shakespeare

A Christmas Carol, The Chimes, A Child's Dream of a Star, Charles Dickens

Gulliver's Travels, Jonathan Swift

The Wind in the Willows, Kenneth Grahame

The Hobbit, The Lord of the Rings, The Silmarillion, The Children of Hurin, JRR Tolkien

The Chronicles of Narnia, CS Lewis

The works of Jasper Fforde

Watership Down, Richard Adams

The Worst Witch series, Jill Murphy

The Harry Potter series, JK Rowling

The Eragon quartet, Christopher Paolini

Alice's Adventures in Wonderland, Lewis Carroll

Artemis Fowl, Eoin Colfer

Inkheart, Cornelia Funke

The Neverending Story, Michael Ende

Peter Pan, JM Barrie

The Happy Prince, The Nightingale and the Rose, The Selfish Giant, The Picture of Dorian Gray, Oscar Wilde

His Dark Materials trilogy, *The Scarecrow and his Servant*, Philip Pullman

The Wonderful Wizard of Oz, L Frank Baum

The Pied Piper of Hamelin, Robert Browning

Weaveworld, The Thief of Always, Clive Barker

Coraline, Death: The High Cost of Living, the Sandman series, Neil Gaiman

Glory Road, Robert A Heinlein

Solomon Kane, the Conan novels, Robert E Howard

The Lost World, Sir Arthur Conan Doyle

The Land That Time Forgot, Edgar Rice Burroughs

King Kong, Edgar Wallace and Merian C Cooper [Delos W Lovelace]

Complete works, the Brothers Grimm
Brer Rabbit, Uncle Remus
Just So Stories, Rudyard Kipling
Duncton Wood, Duncton Quest, Duncton Found, Duncton Tales,
Duncton Rising, Duncton Stone, William Horwood

About the Author

Craig Cabell is the author of 16 books. He has been a freelance writer and reporter for over 20 years, working most notably for the *Independent*. For five years he was a rock journalist and then an in-house reporter for *Focus*, the House Journal of the Ministry of Defence, where he wrote many articles and news features. He has written both book and wine reviews for several different magazines and has travelled the world for government services. He was part of the rebuilding of Kuwait after the first Gulf War but more recently has helped UK small businesses succeed in the United States of America. He is the author of the acclaimed *Operation Big Ben – The anti-V2 Spitfire Missions, 1944–45* with Graham A Thomas, which was made into a CGI film and spawned limited edition models of the clipped-winged Mark XVI Spitfires used in the operation. His book *VE Day – A Day to Remember* with Allan Richards also received much praise and was part of the 60th anniversary of VE Day gala performance in London's Trafalgar Square, where

Richard E Grant acted reminiscences from veterans detailed in the book. Cabell lives in London with his wife, three children, and lots of Terry Pratchett books, and wishes that one day he has enough time on his hands to get bored.

Books by Craig Cabell

Frederick Forsyth – A Matter of Protocol, the Authorised Biography
The Kray Brothers – The Image Shattered
James Herbert – Devil in the Dark, the Authorised True Story
Operation Big Ben – The anti-V2 Spitfire Missions 1944–45
(with Graham A Thomas)
VE Day – A Day to Remember (with Allan Richards)
Snipers (with Richard Brown)
Dennis Wheatley – Churchill's Storyteller
Getting Away With Murder (with Lenny Hamilton)
Witchfinder General – the Biography of Matthew Hopkins
Ian Fleming's Secret War – Author of James Bond
The History of 30 Assault Unit – Ian Fleming's Red Indians
Captain Kidd – The Hunt for the Truth (with Graham A
Thomas & Allan Richards)
The Hunt for Blackbeard (with Graham A Thomas & Allan
Richards)
Ian Rankin and Inspector Rebus

CRAIG CABELL

The Doctors Who's Who

Terry Pratchett — The Spirit of Fantasy

CHAP BOOKS

Dennis Wheatley and the Occult

Black Sniper (fiction)

I was Alive Then — The Spike Milligan Interviews

The Grapes of MoD — Ten years of wine consumption

30 Assault Unit User Manual

Why Did I Invite Them Round to Tea (fiction)

Tales of Verona

The Curse of the Baskervilles

William — The Story of a Royal Marine

*Robert A Heinlein — The Complete UK Bibliography
and Collector's Guide*

*Stephen King — The Complete UK Bibliography
and Collector's Guide*

Ian Rankin Illustrated UK Bibliography and Collector's Guide

A Christmas Vampire (fiction)

The Arms Dealers Arms

Stories with Wine

SPECIAL INTRODUCTIONS

*Furies Over Korea — The story of the men of the Fleet Air Arm,
RAF and Commonwealth who defended South Korea, 1950–1953*
by Graham A Thomas

Firestorm, Typhoons Over Caen, 1944 by Graham A Thomas

Terror from the Sky — The Battle Against the Flying Bomb by
Graham A Thomas

*The Dan Brown Enigma — The Biography of the world's greatest
thriller writer* by Graham A Thomas